The
Humanist
as Traveler

The Humanist as Traveler

George Sandys's *Relation of a Journey begun An. Dom. 1610*

Jonathan Haynes

Rutherford • Teaneck • Madison
Fairleigh Dickinson University Press
London and Toronto: Associated University Presses

© 1986 by Associated University Presses, Inc.

Associated University Presses
440 Forsgate Drive
Cranbury, NJ 08512

Associated University Presses
25 Sicilian Avenue
London WC1A 2QH, England

Associated University Presses
2133 Royal Windsor Drive
Unit 1
Mississauga, Ontario
Canada L5J 1K5

Library of Congress Cataloging-in-Publication Data
Haynes, Jonathan.
    The humanist as traveler.

    Bibliography: p.
    Includes index.
    1. Sandys, George, 1578–1644. Relation of a journey begun an. dom. 1610.   2. Sandys, George, 1578–1644—Near East.   3. Sandys, George, 1578–1644—Journeys—Italy.   4. Near East—Description and travel.   5. Italy—Description and travel—1501–1800.   6. Renaissance—England.   I. Title.
    DS47.S23H39   1986   915.6′041   84-46112
    ISBN 0-8386-3240-8 (alk. paper)

Printed in the United States of America

to my parents

Contents

Acknowledgments

The greatest debt I have incurred in producing this study is to Thomas M. Greene, who, when it began its existence as a dissertation at Yale, was its director. It is a debt that needs to be acknowledged here all the more emphatically because it is not reflected in my footnotes; but anyone familiar with his work on humanism and historical awareness in the Renaissance will find abundant evidence of his influence in what follows. ". . . a grateful mind / By owing owes not, but still pays, at once / Indebted and discharg'd."

The American University in Cairo provided me with a grant which supported further research and revisions and generally made me welcome and helped to educate me during my years there. I am particularly grateful to Doris E.-C. Shoukri. Thanks also to Albion College for a grant which covered production costs of the manuscript.

My readers should be grateful to Louis L. Martz, without whose advice what follows would be more painful and less profitable to read. I am pleased to remember the encouragement he gave me at several crucial stages. I want to thank the friends and teachers who read parts or all of the manuscript: Eugene Waith, Dorothee Metlitzki, Joseph Loewenstein, David Konstan, Robert Mankin, John Rieder, Christopher Kendrick, Victoria Kahn, Reed Dasenbrock, and my father, Thomas M. Haynes. Finally, thanks to Ann Duerr for technical assistance.

VERITAS

CONSTANTIA

SIC REDIBIT

MONS OLIVARVM

MAGNAE ESTIS ET PRAEVALEBITIS

ACHMET, SIVE TYRANNVS

ISIS, SIVE ÆGYPTVS

A
RELATION
of a Iourney begun
Añ: Dom: 1610.

FOVRE BOOKES.

Containing, a description of
the Turkish Empire, of Ægypt,
of the Holy Land, of the Remote parts of Italy,
and Ilands ad-
ioyning.

LONDON.

Printed for W: Barrett.
1615.

VICTA IACET

SIBYLLA CVMRA

FOLIISQVE NOTAS ET NOMINA MANDAT

APIS SIVE OSIRIS

Title page from the first edition, 1615. *(By permission of the Houghton Library, Harvard University.)*

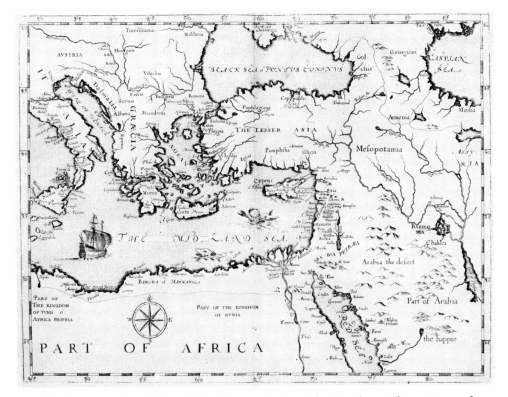

Map from the first edition, 1615. *(By permission of the Houghton Library, Harvard University.)*

Introduction

This book has two main purposes: to resurrect a minor classic of the English Renaissance; and to reflect on Renaissance modes of thinking about history and culture. George Sandys added to the account of his travels around the eastern Mediterranean a wealth of historical and geographical materials, and enough interspersed poetic translations to give the whole a thoroughly literary flavor, even to make it appear as a kind of geographically organized Florilegium. The result is an attempt to represent as fully and as authoritatively as possible the significance for an educated 17th century Englishman of this densest of all landscapes. The origins of our civilization are there: Judeo-Christian and Greco-Roman, of course, and we can feel Sandys groping after the lost civilizations of Egypt, Phoenecia, and Crete. It was also the scene of the confrontation with Islam, which for the Renaissance was the central instance of cultural otherness, a direct military, religious, and cultural threat which bore on the European mind much more powerfully than the newly discovered cultures of the New World. And English merchants were active in the Levant, and English diplomacy was trying to exploit tensions between the Ottomans and Persians, and it was already clear that the Levant lay on the way to India. The *Relation* ambitiously and successfully responds to all these interests, and tries to read all these cultures, interpret all these histories.

Sandys and his book stand squarely at the conjunction of two great historical events: the consolidation of humanist culture in England and the foundation of the British Empire. These two themes, along with a stout Anglican orthodoxy which embraces both of them, run through Sandys's family history and biography as through the *Relation*.[1] He was born in March 1577/8, the year Drake set sail on his circumnavigation, probably also the year Richard Hakluyt gave the first lectures on geography at Oxford.[2] His father Edwin was successively Vice-Chancellor of Cambridge, a houseguest of Peter Martyr's during the Marian persecution, a translator of the Bishop's Bible, and Archbishop of York. George Clifford, the privateering Earl of Cumberland, stood as George's godfather. George's older brother Sir Edwin was a friend and literary executor of Richard Hooker, and a friend of the great Venetian historian Fra Paolo Sarpi, who translated his *Survey of the State of Religion in the Westerne Parts of the World*. He became a leader in Parliament and was active in the East India

Company and, more importantly, in the Virginia Company, which he dominated through much of its life as the head of a faction composed largely of his
numerous brothers and cousins.[3]

George Sandys was educated at Oxford and the Middle Temple, where he
was contemporary with a brilliant group of wits and writers including Sir
Henry Wotton, John Davies, John Marson, and Thomas Overbury.[4] After the
journey begun in 1610 and the publication of the *Relation* in 1615 he began
work on his great translation and commentary on Ovid; this work was continued during his residence in the Virginia Colony as its energetic Treasurer, as
Michael Drayton urged him:

> And (worthy GEORGE) by industry and use,
> Let's see what lines *Virginia* will produce;
> Goe on with Ovid, as you have begunne,
> With the first five Bookes; let your numbers run
> Glib as the former, so shall it live long,
> And doe much honour to the *English* tongue:
> Intice the Muses thither to repaire,
> Intreat them gently, trayne them to that ayre . . .[5]

The image of Sandys creating the first English poetry in the New World while
busy trying to establish new industries and leading punitive raids against the
Indians complements perfectly the sense of cultural mission that informs the
Relation. Later he became an advisor on colonial affairs to the Privy Council,
and settled into a devout old age, publishing paraphrases of the poetical parts of
the Bible and a translation of Hugo Grotius's *Christ's Passion*. The link with
Grotius is significant: Sandys was a fixture in Falkland's circle at Great Tew,
where Grotius and his Arminianism were greatly admired; and if, as is very
likely, he maintained his family's connection with Sarpi while in Venice, he can
be associated directly with the two principal figures in the international Eras-
mian humanism of the generation before the Thirty Years War.[6]

Sandys had the talent as well as the background for the vast act of cultural
memory and will which is the *Relation*. The learning he displays there
foreshadows the massive erudition of his *Ovid,* and his contemporaries considered him one of the major literary talents of the day. Both the *Relation* and
the *Ovid* went through many editions and traces of the *Relation* have been
found in works by Bacon, Burton, Browne, Cowley, Thomas Fuller, Jonson,
and Milton, among others. Very much later when a young clergyman asked Dr.
Johnson for advice on his education, Johnson provided him with a short reading list on which we find "Sandys' *Travels*" between Sprat's *History of the
Royal Society* and *The Compleate Angler*.[7] Henry Lawes thought well enough
of his paraphrases of the Psalms to set them twice (1638 and 1648), and they
were one of the books King Charles had with him immediately before his
execution. Many of the members of the Great Tew circle contributed commendatory poems to the first edition of the Psalms. A lot of what was said about

him, especially in the commendatory poems, now seems extravagant, but at the end of the century Dryden still remembered him as "the ingenious and learned Sandys, the best versifier of the former age."[8]

The *Relation* set a new standard for English travel literature, in its depth and accuracy, and in its formality. This formality is not simply a matter of literary finish, though it is that too: more importantly it demonstrates an ability to give form to the foreign and the past, in a deliberate and comprehensive way, to appropriate great tracts of cultural history and deliver them to the English reader. The ability and need to do this is symptomatic of the maturing of English culture, the sense that England ought to have the world in which it was becoming a major actor represented to it with proper sophistication and rhetorical pomp. Most of this study is devoted to exploring the cultural forms which underlie Sandys's formalities.

The full title of Sandys's book is *A Relation of a Iourney begun An: Dom: 1610. Foure Bookes. Containing a description of the Turkish Empire, of AEgypt, of the Holy Land, of the Remote parts of Italy, and Ilands adioyning.* On the title page the title itself is surrounded by an elaborate engraving by Francis Delaram displaying allegorical figures who represent the places Sandys visited. The figures are arranged around an architectural edifice of ambiguous genre—temple, theater, or triumphal arch—but of a definitely classical style; the figures are fully modeled and finely engraved, and the whole composition is clear and well proportioned, not as congested as such title pages usually are. The allegory is open and urbane. Sandys doubtless collaborated with the artist on it, as he did on the engravings for *Ovid's Metamorphosis Englished, Mythologized, and Represented in Figures.*

To the left of the title stands a figure in rich Turkish dress, identified by a sign on the pillar behind as *"Achmet, sive tyrannus"*: the Turkish Sultan. In his left hand he holds the orb of the world, and in his right a yoke; he is trampling on a couple of learned-looking tomes and a scale. On the other side of the title, before the opposing pillar, stands *"Isis, sive AEgyptus"*. She is laden with objects bespeaking the ancient mysteries of Egypt: perhaps she represents the origins of civilization, as Achmet represents its scourge if not its end. One suspects an English girl stood as the model for this figure, who is rendered in the classical style of the other figures rather than in that of ancient Egyptian art.

In the center below the title is a lozenge showing the Cumaean Sibyl sitting before her cave, with the Virgilian inscription *"foliisque notas et nomina mandat"*. She is a mild virgin, more apt to sing the prophecies of Christ than to be possessed by the furors of Apollo. Centered above the title is another lozenge in which her prophecy is fulfilled: Christ hovers in a blaze of glory above the Mount of Olives, transcending the hills of Palestine below him, which seem to have been scorched bare by his fiery ascent. The Redeemer is flanked by the guardian angels of Christian humanism, Veritas and Constantia. Veritas is of course naked, or as naked as modesty permits; she holds a book in her lap, along with an enormous quill pen. In her other hand she holds the sun, and she directs her clear gaze towards the risen Christ, or perhaps past him to her sister Constantia. Constantia is helmeted and wears a mailed shirt emblazoned with a cross; she holds a flame in one hand, and with the other arm embraces a pillar. Her eyes are downcast a little sadly; she seems to be contemplating Sultan Achmet below her and to the left. But on the lintel which supports the upper figures is inscribed the legend "magnae estis et praevalebitis".

The engraving is a fine expression of the contents of the book, and of the allegorical and symbolic imagination behind it. The figures represent great powers in the history of the West, figures of mystery and danger as well as of human values and divine promise. They come out of very different times and places, and the attempt to render them all in the same artistic language creates some stylistic anachronisms, but they are all integrated into a coherent composition. The classical masonry binds them together and creates the framework in which thematic relations are set up. Four books, four countries, four personifications, each out of a different tradition: this is the scheme of the *Relation.*

The symbolic plan is crucial, but its formative power usually works below the surface, while the book more overtly makes itself responsible to an exacting standard of geographical knowledge. The map of the eastern Mediterranean is as handsome as the title page, and it is quite accurate, its sophisticated cartography reflecting a mature geographical science. There is a compass rose, and latitude and longitude markings guarantee that space has been measured and controlled. The sea monsters are merely ornamental, and they share the waters of the Mid-Land Sea with a merchant ship sailing purposefully towards the east.

The land forms are perfectly solid, but assigning legends reflects some cultural peculiarities. The map nowhere recognizes Turkish or Arab jurisdiction— "The lesser Asia" is still divided into territories called Phrygia, Lydia, and the rest, and the Levant into Phoenicia, Galilee, and so on. One might conclude (with justice) that the Muslim presence was thought of as a shadow over the land rather than as an historical actuality to be assimilated; but it should also be remembered that most readers of the *Relation* had their sense of geography formed by an education in the classics and the Bible, which left an abiding interest in the ancient places. The modern places one would want to know about, for trade or other reasons, were placed within this framework. As one gets further east (the map reaches to Media and Assyria) interest in the modern decreases, and the map increasingly reverts to ancient names. "Babilon" is on the map, but Baghdad is not. Not a map for mariners or merchants, then, but for an educated reader seeking general knowledge. The map represents neither the ancient nor the modern worlds, but the interests of its readers, and the world Sandys describes.

The integration of past and present into a general vision of what was significant about the lands of the eastern Mediterranean is characteristic of the book as a whole: in fact it is the point of the book, as Sandys tells us in his dedication to Prince Charles. The dedication is worth quoting in full, as it contains the most concentrated expression of Sandys's themes and purposes; it is also a splendid example of his rhetorical powers.

Sir,

The Eminence of the degree wherein God and Nature haue placed you, doth allure the eyes; and the hopefulness of your Vertues, win the loue of all men. For Vertue being in a priuate person an exemplary ornament; aduanceth it selfe in a Prince to be a publike blessing. And as the Sunne to the world, so bringeth it both light and life to a kingdome: a light of direction, by glorious example; and a life of ioy, through a gracious gouernement. From the iust and serious consideration whereof, there springeth in minds not brutish, a thankfull correspondence of affection and duty; still pressing to expresse themselues in endeauours of service. Which also hath caused me, (most noble Prince) not furnished of better meanes, to offer in humble zeale to your princely view these my double trauels; once with some toyle and danger performed, and now recorded with sincerity and diligence. The parts I speake of are the most renowned countries and kingdomes: once the seats of most glorious and triumphant Empires; the theaters of valour and heroicall actions; the soiles enriched with all earthly felicities; the places where Nature hath produced her wonderfull works; where Arts and Sciences haue bene inuented, and perfited; where wisedome, vertue, policie, and ciuility haue bene planted, haue flourished: and lastly where God himselfe did place his owne Commonwealth, gaue lawes and oracles, inspired his Prophets, sent Angels to conuerse with men; above all, where the Sonne of God descended to become man; where he honoured the earth with his beautifull steps, wrought the worke of our redemption, triumphed ouer death, and ascended into glory. Which countries once so glorious, and famous for their happy estate, are now through vice and ingratitude, become the most deplored spectacles of extreme miserie: the wilde beasts of mankind hauing broken in vpon them, and rooted out all ciuilitie; and the pride of a sterne and barbarous Tyrant possessing the thrones of ancient and iust dominion. Who aiming onely at the height of greatnesse and sensuality, hath in tract of time reduced so great and so goodly a part of the world, to that lamentable distresse and servitude, vnder which (to the astonishment of the vnderstanding beholders) it now faints and groneth. Those rich lands at this present remain wast and ouergrowne with bushes, receptacles of wild beats, of theeues, and murderers; large territories dispeopled, or thinly inhabited; goodly cities made desolate; sumptuous buildings become ruines; glorious Temples either subuerted, or prostituted to impietie; true religion discountenanced and oppressed; all Nobility extinguished; no light of learning permitted, nor Vertue cherished: violence and rapine insulting ouer all, and leauing no security saue to an abiect mind, and vnlookt on pouerty. Which calamities of theirs so great and deserued, are to the rest of the world as threatning instructions. For assistance wherein, I haue not onely related what I saw of their present condition; but so far as conueniency might permit, presented a briefe view of the former estates, and first antiquities of those peoples and countries: thence to draw a right image of the frailty of man, and mutability of what so ever is worldly; and assurance that as there is nothing vnchangeable sauing God, so nothing stable but his grace and protection. Accept great Prince these weake endeauours of a strong desire: which shall be alwaies deuoted to do your Highnesse all acceptable seruice; and euer reioyce in your prosperity and happinesse.

George Sandys

In his vision of civilization as something glorious and heroic, in his faith in human powers mingled with a Christian recognition of man's frailty, in the appeal to a benign natural law of harmony and correspondences, in his belief in the continuity of private and public virtues and in the power of rhetoric to express and bind them together, and in his preoccupation with historical achievement and historical loss, Sandys shows us English humanism in its fullest flowering. History is displayed to us as a moral spectacle, illustrating a simple paradigm: a happy state is violated by sin, and retribution follows. The historian's role is moral and rhetorical, to deliver "threatening instructions" gleaned from contemplating the ruins of time. Again and again the beautifully controlled rhythms of Sandys's prose mark the passage from weal into woe.

This is history at a very high level of abstraction: the ruins are vivid enough, but there are no dates or proper names. Sandys knows them all, and will prove himself a master of all the historical arts of the humanist, but here he is concerned to show the pattern the names and dates will articulate. One might also say that this is history at a very simple level of abstraction: and indeed a few grand terms do provide the basic framework. But it will be the burden of Part II of this study to show that Sandys saw not one uniform history but a series of pasts, each of which brought with it a different concept of what history was, and a different hermeneutic. As I shall show in the last chapter, when he returns to Italy Sandys will display the sense of the past we would expect from a northern humanist. But our humanist travels further afield; his humanism is tested and stretched. Muslim history is completely outside the purview of the dedication, except as the scourge of God: "the wild beasts of mankind hauing broken in . . . . and rooted out all ciuilitie; and the pride of a sterne and barbarous Tyrant possessing the thrones of ancient and iust dominion." "Achmet, sive tyrannus"; and Muhammad represents an analogous spiritual tyranny: Muslim culture is systemmatically condemned on theological grounds which leave very little room for the sense of human creativity in history the humanists felt informing their own past.

Egyptian history was unimaginably long, and no one knew how to read its records: the learning the Renaissance had to apply to ancient Egypt was nearly all tinged with Hermeticism, and Hermeticism represents the most spectacular failure of the new philology of the humanists, and the approach to history it fostered. Sandys was no Hermeticist, but what he does in Egypt has more to do with the interpretation of emblems than with the careful differentiation of historical epochs. Like the figure of Isis, his Egypt is anachronistic if also wonderfully symbolic. It is in the Holy Land, as one might expect, that the theme of sin and retribution finds its strongest expression. The blaze of divine glory came and went in the history of Palestine, leaving it scarred; a Protestant anxiety about mingling the spiritual and the material keeps Christ hovering above the land, out of touch with it. The Jews murdered him, the Catholics have falsified his memory—history is the history of unworthiness. Rome fell for good, but quite different reasons.

It has been persuasively argued that Renaissance humanism invented the modern concepts of history and culture.[9] Through the attempt to revive classical antiquity the humanists discovered historical difference: they noticed the anachronism in painting Cicero or the tormentors of Christ in Renaissance costume, and founded the discipline of philology, dedicated to differentiating epochs and cultures from each other. Culture came to be seen as an integral whole, evolving over time, making a history of culture possible and necessary. It is through such a history of culture that the humanist hermeneutic operates, communication taking place across a sympathetic recognition of difference. By implication all cultures share the dignity of having their own character and history, the patient explication of which will make cross-cultural communication possible.

It is a great and noble idea, as great as any idea the West has contributed to a world civilization. A less noble form of the same idea, the ability to systematically and cynically master and manipulate a foreign symbol system, has been discussed by Stephen Greenblatt;[10] this ability is partly responsible for the rise of the West to world dominion. And Edward Said has written eloquently about the ways in which the human sciences, including those fostered by humanism, can be employed and distorted by the institutions of power, the hermeneutical impulse being seriously qualified if not dispensed with in the process.[11] The history of the idea, then, is far from simple, and can hardly be taken too seriously.

Sandys offers us the opportunity for an exemplary case study—not because he solved all the problems of cultural understanding, but because the range of his experiences and the depth of his learning make him a responsible figure, one who can withstand our questioning. Much of what follows will have to do with the natural and inevitable failures of historical and cultural understanding, measured against the pure standard of the humanists' revival of the classical world. Often these failures can be explained in terms of something like natural laws: understanding another culture in its integrity and specificity is an immense amount of work, even when there is no serious language barrier, and there is nothing surprising in the unwillingness or inability to make such an investment; it is natural to see a culture that is different from one's own as being a distortion of one's own; one is apt to see what is already expected or familiar; it is easier to take a cultural detail out of context and give it an emblematic significance through one's own interpretative procedures than to reconstruct its original context; and so on. But Sandys's failures and his many successes are also deeply rooted in the specific historical situation in which he traveled and wrote.

The humanist ideas of culture and history developed unevenly and slowly. If by implication the ideas developed in the study of antiquity applied to other cultures, in practice they did so incompletely and irregularly. In large part the complexity and irregularity of the patterns in which the foreign presented itself to Sandys are the result of the relative weakness of Renaissance theories of culture, of what we would call the social or human sciences. We look to the Renaissance for the beginning (or revival) of such theories in a number of fields—history, political science, ethnology, demography, and others—but they were as yet new, rudimentary in form and limited in scope, preoccupied with the European experience (including that of antiquity) to the exclusion of other cultures. When faced with interpreting the meaning of a foreign culture a man as conservative as Sandys would still be guided less by a theory or set of theories than by a tradition associated with that culture, a collection of received interpretations, literary representations, attitudes, interests, stereotypes, *topoi*, and so on, based not on a theoretical paradigm but on what I will be calling an historical myth. There were a number of such traditions, and in spite of centuries of coexistence and syncretic interpretation they were still not wholly aligned with each other.

The tension arising from conflicts between the Judeo-Christian and classical traditions is of course the most important. In the Commentary on Ovid, Sandys clearly states the primacy of the truth of the Bible and employs various techniques bequeathed him by previous commentators to subordinate the classical heritage to the Hebraic: the figures of pagan mythology are the figures of the Old Testament in disguise, and in his account of the creation Ovid appears "so consonant to the truth, as doubtlesse he had either seene the Books of *Moses,* or receaved that doctrine by tradition" (p. 49). But in the *Relation* this subordination and the interpretative methods through which it is effected are much less apparent. The world of the *Relation* is a much less coherent place; it has a number of centers of gravity, as it were, and different places are governed by different laws which sometimes contradict each other. A nice illustration of this relativity is Sandys's employment of several different chronological schemes. Following Eusebius and Scaliger (they disagree slightly) he can date the fall of Troy by a "yeare of the world" and link it to a contemporary event in Old Testament history (p. 20), but he will date other events by Olympiads (p. 244) or by the founding of Rome (p. 288). The science of chronology is still too weak to break down several pasts into one uniform system. In a somewhat equivalent manner even the theme of historical loss is just that, a theme and not a theory: it means one things in Jerusalem and something very different in Italy.

A further disjunction in Renaissance thinking about culture exists in the gap between the ideas about culture arising from the dialogue with antiquity and the enormous amount of information being gathered about contemporary foreigners as a result of increased trading and the voyages of discovery. The slowness with which this information was assimilated into the intellectual life of Europe has often been commented on. To a great extent the ancients provided the forms in which this new ethnographical information was collected and presented, but as John Howland Rowe has pointed out, there was a nearly total division between Renaissance theory of social organization (a science by and for Europeans and their ancient ancestors) and ethnography.[12]

The Islamic world was in some respects a special case. It was neither ancient nor new, and it had always been first and foremost a religious issue. Book 1 of the *Relation*, which deals with Islam in general as well as with Turkey and the Turks, is thoroughly shaped by the Christian polemic against Islam. This book contains a fairly elaborate theory of Turkish culture, but it is not easily assimilated to a universal, secular, uniform theory of culture. Sandys did not want an anthropology or history that was simply an intellectual system and not also a religious and moral one.

The religious element in Sandys's thought always has a part to play, but it is not always the same part. In Turkey he is the exponent of a unified and militant Christendom; in Egypt he is more relaxed and Platonizing; in the Holy Land his Protestantism is in the foreground; in Italy his Christian values are implicit and more general. And sometimes religious considerations are less forceful in his thinking than the current political situation or a body of historical memories, especially those connected with the writers of classical antiquity. The intellectual configurations of the *Relation* shift as Sandys shifts his ground. Basic assumptions about the nature of man, of culture, and of history underlie these configurations but have no very stable identity apart from them, so that they too change shape. Not only are the meanings of places and cultures different, but also the processes of establishing those meanings. There is no uniform method for reading and interpreting the foreign.

It should be clear that the principle by which various regions of the Mediterranean landscape emit their own peculiar kinds of meaning has little to do with the sympathetic reconstructions of an historicist or the cultural relativism of an anthropologist. The principle has rather to do with facets, and even contradictions, of Sandys's own culture being activated. In hands as capable as his, travel literature could become a screen on which all the richness and confusion of his culture were projected—a strong form of a general feature of social signification, as James Boon argues:

In the terms employed by structuralists, social facts represent selections from larger sets of possibilities of which societies keep symbolic track, whether consciously or unconsciously, explicity or covertly. Societies conceptualize themselves as select (in both senses) arrangements, valued against contrary arrangements that are in some way "objectified."[13]

Islam is the objectified contrary arrangement in the sharpest and starkest sense, the interpretive principle being one of absolute difference. The roots of Sandys's culture in Egypt or Palestine both are and are not his—there are no simple gestures of embrace or rejection. Onto Roman culture, which is most clearly recognized as his own, an internal opposition (civilization/vice) is projected.

Part II will explore these interpretative strategies: each of its four chapters describes one of the four Books of the *Relation*, and defines the distinctive hermeneutic operating within it. Part I sets Sandys's book in the historical context of the travel genre, and provides a general literary analysis of the *Relation*.

The
Humanist
as Traveler

PART I
Travel and Literature

1

The Development of Travel Literature in England

The intertwined genres of travel and geographical literature were revolutionized in Sandys's lifetime: like the English Renaissance as a whole, they developed with incredible speed and in some confusion. Part of the development concerns the confluence of travel writing with a wider literary culture, but there was a general question of how to write about the foreign and travel experiences which was taken up deliberately by the sponsors of the voyages of discovery, by a new generation of professional geographers, and by educators, as well as by literary men. Together they reformulated the purposes and notions of authority and authorship at work in travel literature, with results that are important for understanding Sandys.

England came late to the overseas expansion of its material and intellectual interests: in the Dedication to the first (1589) edition of his *Principal Navigations* Richard Hakluyt complained that other nations accused England of sluggish neglect of maritime enterprise, and that no one had bothered to publish what had in fact been done and written. Before Hakluyt the field is fairly barren; what there was varied wildly in quality, and most of it was imported from abroad.

There were, to begin with, what Hakluyt called "those wearie volumes bearing the titles of universal Cosmography."[1] Perhaps the most widely known of these books was Sebastian Muenster's *Cosmography* (1550), part of which appeared in English in 1561, and the rest in 1572. It is hard to imagine a work more regressive intellectually—it is essentially similar to medieval encyclopedic works like Bartholomaeus's *De proprietatibus rerum* of 300 years before, containing short descriptions of each country (digested from the geographers of late antiquity and the Middle Ages, such as Solinus and Isidore, who were themselves degenerate epigones of Pliny, Strabo, and Diodorus Siculus), along with stereotypes of the physical and moral character of each people. Johann Boemus's *Omnium gentium mores* (1520), which was translated in bits between 1554 and 1580, and finally in full in 1611, has a slightly different plan, being taken up solely with customs and institutions, but it mined the same sources and has the same character. Both books go on digesting information that was a millenium and a half out of date: in Boemus the Parthians still live between Media and Hyrcania, and Pliny's Troglodites still inhabit Africa along with the Garamantes; the description of Egypt is of ancient Egypt only, the tense of the verbs wobbling back and forth unsteadily between past and present.

Now clearly Boemus's purpose is to present an array of customs, manners, laws, and institutions that are especially worthy to be known, or especially strange—it is an array of possibilities to be contemplated, and it does not greatly matter whether the actualities are gone or were always imaginary. Still the naiveté of the book is astonishing, and reflects the isolation of the learned geographical tradition from the considerable practical knowledge merchants and missionaries had accumulated during the Middle Ages. This isolation is extremely important, and by no means ended with the beginning of the Renaissance. One explanation for it is that knowledge of the non-European world was often carefully kept secret for commercial or strategic reasons, and so was kept out of print or out of writing altogether. One thinks of the massive documentation on the New World kept locked away in Seville. Hakluyt's great publishing venture is doubtless to be explained by the fact that, unlike in Spain where discovery, trade, and colonization were organized and controlled by the Crown through its own bureaucracy, in England overseas expansion was supported by ad hoc groups of investors: City magnates, landed gentry, courtiers, and the Crown. Hakluyt was trying to create an educated public, enthusiastic about such ventures—a new readership, whose interests were not merely contemplative, or who, if they read for amusement or general knowledge, would still want to feel that their reading was related to the real and stirring world of spectacular voyages and wars with the Turk. Geographical knowledge had to be refocused in a new public domain, in the light of both England's new material interests and the intellectual standards sponsored by the new learning.

That Boemus could still be taken seriously enough to be newly translated in the year of Sandys's trip shows how uneven the standards were. There was much to undo as well as much to do. The learned occupied themselves with recovering the ancient geographers who had been badly mangled or forgotten, and with providing them with commentaries. At its best, as in Hakluyt and Sandys, Renaissance geography went about the work of recovering and rectifying ancient knowledge and assimilating the new as part of one process. Hakluyt's lectures on geography at Oxford began with Ptolemy and then proceeded to the modern knowledge that rendered him inadequate.

The rudimentary state of knowledge in an England that was largely ignorant of and indifferent to geography was in great contrast to the works of first-rate intelligence and sophistication being produced on the Continent in the second half of the 16th century, but translations of these works greatly accelerated the advance of geography in England. Hakluyt was in contact with the great geographers and cartographers Mercator and Ortelius. Giovanni Botero's *Relationi universali* (1597; translated in 1601 by Robert Johnson as *The Travellers Breviat*) was a cosmography written from a completely new intellectual perspective. It is dedicated to an exploration of the principles of political and military organization with reference to geography and climate. History is considered as a product of these forces, and the traditional forms of historical knowledge (battles, dynasties, and so on) are dispensed with. Similarly Jean Bodin (*Methodus ad Facilem Historiarum Cognitionem*, 1566) brought history, geography, politics and ethnology into contact with each other in his plan for a history that would be based on scientific principles and would be genuinely universal in scope. He was widely known and influential in England, though usually in modified and unscientific terms through Du Bartas.[2] We might also mention Louis le Roy (or Regius), whose *De La Vicissitude ou varieté des choses en l'universe* (1575; translated by Robert Ashley, 1594) shows a serious interest in comparative history.[3]

These books were read in England, by George Sandys among others, but it was a long time before England produced any comparable work of synthetic intelligence—perhaps the first is Edward Brerewood's *Enquiries touching the Diversity of Languages and Religions through the Chief Parts of the World*, published posthumously in 1614. But by this time competent and mature work was being produced in a variety of related fields. Sandys's *Relation*, published a year after Brerewood's *Enquiries*, will be our main exhibit; Samuel Purchas's *Purchas his Pilgrimage, Or Relations of the World and the Religions Observed in all ages and places discouered, from the Creation vnto this present* appeared the year before, and was wider in scope that anything that had yet been written. This is also the period of the great surveys of English history by Camden, Speed, and Stow. The first, and already massive, edition of Richard Knolles's *Generall History of the Turkes* had appeared in 1603, attesting to a serious interest in the history of at least one non-European nation. And in 1612 Peter Heylyn published *Microcosmus, or A Little Description of the Great World. A Treatise Historicall, Geographicall, Politicall, Theologicall*, a competent and even elegant cosmography which drew on all the works we have just mentioned, as well as on the ancients and on George Sandys and other travellers of his generation. (A greatly expanded version was published in 1652 as *Cosmographie. In Foure Bookes*; two years earlier another churchman idled by the Civil War had published another massive work of historical geography, Thomas Fuller's *Pisgahsight of Palestine*.) English geography had come of age.

As for published travel literature in England before Hakluyt, there was not a great deal. There were some old pilgrimage narratives, some new accounts of the Muscovie Company, Drake, Gilbert, and Frobisher, and an ephemeral literature, often in the form of broadsides and ballads, describing sea fights or wars with the Turks. There was little narrative literature of the caliber of the works being translated into English, such as those by Peter Martyr (translated in 1555 by Richard Eden, with additions), Thevet (1568), Varthema (1577), Cartier (1580), Nicholas de Nicolay (1585), Pigafetta (1585), or Cesare Federici (1588). A new era begins with Hakluyt's publication first of the 1589 *Principal Navigations* and then of the three big folios of the same title in 1598–1600.

Richard Hakluyt is undoubtedly the most important historical figure in the development I am outlining, as George Bruner Parks has shown.[4] He and his older cousin, distinguished as Richard Hakluyt of the Middle Temple, were the first professional geographers in England. The relationships among travel literature, the explorations, and commercial interests are all expressed in his career. But I am interested here only in his role in the development of travel literature. In the preface "To the favourable Reader" in the first edition he explains his method:

> And to the ende that those men which were the payneful and personall travellers might reape that good opinion and just commendation which they have deserved, and further, that every man might answere for himselfe, justifie his reports, and stand accountable for his owne doings, I have referred every voyage to his Author, which both in person hath performed, and in writing hath left the same: for I am not ignorant of Ptolemies assertion, that *Peregrinationis historia,* and not those wearie volumes bearing the titles of universall Cosmography which some men that I could name have published as their owne, beying in deed most untruly and unprofitablie ramassed and hurled together, is that which must bring us to the certayne and full discoverie of the world.[5]

It might be noticed to begin with that his purposes are not literary. Certainly his overall purposes were in great part, perhaps overwhelmingly, propagandistic and hence rhetorical. He could turn his own considerable literary gifts to the evocation of the heroic experiences of the voyages if he thought that it would inspire others to the task (see, for instance, I, p. xlii on the Northeastern voyages); and he probably had some sense that he was compiling the "great prose epic" (Froude's phrase) of the Empire that did not yet exist. But his more overt purpose is geographical, and the assumption of the *Principal Navigations* which is expressed here is that if enough works of one kind (travel narratives) are accumulated, a higher form of knowledge (geography) will result. This is the expression of a particular moment in the histories of exploration and of empiricism. Hakluyt has in abundance the empiricist's passion for collecting reliable data, but he is not ready yet to synthesize it into a higher, more abstract form. The whole enterprise still turned on extraordinary individuals operating outside the boundaries of what was known. It was very difficult to control their actions or check their stories.

In any event geographical authority was refounded here, in *Peregrinationis historia* rather than in secondhand and second rate universal cosmography. To refound authority he had to find authors. At first they appear as English subjects brought to a royal court to reap the good opinion and commendation they have deserved, but they are quickly reconstituted as legal subjects in a court of law, who stand as witnesses to be interrogated and presumably prosecuted if their testimony is false or inadequate. The travel writer is suddenly a person of importance and responsibility, a scientific instrument. He will be read critically, and must behave himself appropriately in order to establish his credibility and authority.

The problem Hakluyt faced is clear enough if we remember that in the first edition he prints *Mandeville's Travels* (c 1370), that wonderful compilation of medieval fantasies whose authenticity and authorship are still in doubt. On his way home, Mandeville tells us at the end of his book, he went to Rome and gave his book to the Pope, who showed it to his council, which approved it as true because they had a book that contained everything that was in Mandeville's. And this was exactly the circular system of authentication by which the Middle Ages accepted *Mandeville's Travels:* because he seconded the wildest rumors of Pliny or Vincent of Beauvais, because there was nothing new in him, he must be telling the truth. Compare Marco Polo on his deathbed in Venice, surrounded by friends urging him to retract his stories, for which no authority could be provided.

Or compare the narrative of Friar Beatus Odoricus of a trip to China in 1330, which replaces Mandeville in the second edition of the *Principal Voyages* (Vol. IV, pp. 371–443; Odoric was one of Mandeville's principal sources). Odoric closes with a sworn, dated, and witnessed statement—required by his monastic superior—that everything he said is true. But even this does not solve the problem. Anxiously he repeats again and again:

> Thus much concerning those things which I beheld most certainly with mine eyes, I frier Odoricus have heere written; many strange things also I have of purpose omitted, because men will not beleeve them unless they should see them.[6]

Apart from the question of credibility, Odoric will serve as an example of the poverty-stricken methods of the naive observers Hakluyt had to rely on. There is no attempt to make a country comprehensible in its entirety: Odoric always tells what the food is like, but that is about the extent of his personal involvement with the new environment; and coupled with a marvel or two it will suffice as a complete description. Geographically his route across better-known territory is reasonably clear, but only because the names are already familiar. The reader has to have a map already in mind in order to follow him— it is very difficult to construct one from the text, which does not specify topographical relationships with much care. Of course his readers would not have had a good map to refer to. Nor can Odoric refer to the geographical sense that would be the byproduct of a humanist's classical education; the ancients would have helped him at least across Persia, but he is immediately on his own, trying to create a sense of geography from scratch, and without training. Consequently Odoric is more fascinating than he is useful.

So the task was not simply to locate authors, but to create authors who could be relied on to see everything, to write it down coherently, and to establish their personal credibility so they could be believed even when what they said was new and extraordinary. It would also be desirable if they knew the record and could refer to it—if they understood their relation to previous literature and knowledge. They should be, in a word, responsible, able to respond to the questions likely to be put to them.

The new requirements were institutionalized in various ways. Hakluyt's elder cousin drew up lists of things to be observed by merchants going abroad; these would be organized into formal outlines, like Albrecht Meier's *Certain briefe, and speciall instructions for gentlemen, merchants, students, souldiers, marriners, etc.* (1587; English translation 1589, probably at the younger Hakluyt's request); ultimately the Royal Society would take over the organization and policing of a corps of informants. Robert Boyle set out "General Heads for a Natural History of a Countrey, Great or Small" (*Transactions of the Royal Society* I, p. 186, April 2, 1666), and travelers' reports were reviewed (and sometimes printed) in the *Transactions.*[7] Meanwhile the spirit that produced these schematic headings was embodied in the persons of the trained observers sent along with voyages of discovery. Hakluyt tried to sail to Virginia in this capacity, but Ralegh already had his own scientific consultant and observer, Thomas Hariot. More's Utopia and Bacon's New Atlantis are both equipped with a class of scientific spies.

On a less official plane, there was a large literature of advice for travellers, which usually took the form of headings like Meier's set out in prose, along with some moral advice. A young man setting out would solicit a letter of advice from an older and wiser traveler (many applied to Sir Henry Wotton).[8] Bacon's essay "Of Travel" is such a work in the form of an essay. As the need grew, more and more works of this kind were printed.[9] In 1633 appeared a tiny volume, designed, as its publisher says, to be carried along, called *Profitable Instructions: describing what special observations are to be taken by Travellers in all Nations, States, and Countries.* It contains three items, a schematic outline of heads for observing the geography, people, and government of a country by Secretary William Davidson, and letters by Robert Devereux, Earl of Essex, and Sir Philip Sidney. Essex's letter is a serious discourse on travel as a moral experience, as a trial and an opportunity for growth. Here the analysis is not of the forms under which to observe foreign countries, but of the faculties of the traveler. Sidney's letter (to his younger brother) is a more personal and troubled meditation on the same theme. He complains that he has wasted his opportunity, and admonishes his brother to travel with a serious purpose, namely to furnish himself with knowledge of things serviceable to his country and calling. The figure of the affected English traveler haunts the letter: "wee travellers shall be made sport of in Comedies" (p. 81).[10]

Enough and maybe too much has been written about the Renaissance love of travel: what is needed is a study of the anxieties about it. There were plenty of real dangers (highwaymen, disease, seductive Jesuits, the Inquisition). But apart from fear there was a moral anxiety about travel itself. Many if not most people believed the experience was probably not good for the average man, that it only exposed him to the vicious habits of other countries, to which he was only too prone. The traveler was morally suspect. He had become a highly evolved and negative social stereotype, paraded on stage and pilloried in satires. Partly this was because England did not like what exposure to the Continent did to her young men; their prestige as travelers was resented and their sophistication despised. But the objections went deeper than that. To travel was to give oneself up to mutability, and movement and change were viewed with suspicion in the Renaissance: in a world thought to be decaying, change was synonymous with degeneration. The tower of Babel shows that variety is the mark of sin; the farther Noah's children wandered, the more barbaric they became (the American Indians were most so). Transmission of cultural traits from one people to another was almost always a bad thing. The peoples who could claim never to have moved and never to have changed—the Athenians, the Germans, the Ethiopians—were thought to be best.[11] Many must have thought what was never better expressed than in a dedication by one Richard Wrag:

> If you aske mee what in my travels I have learned, I answere as a noble man of France did to the like demaund, *Hoc unum didici, mundi contemptum*: and so concluding with the wise man in the booke of the Preacher, that all is vanitie, and one thing onely is necessarie, I take my leave and commit you to the Almightie.[12]

We might also remember that social legislation was geared to keeping people at home even within England; and no one could leave England without an exit visa, which could not be obtained without a good reason or good connections or a good deal of money.

In a climate of opinion like this it was an uphill battle to justify travel at all. There was an established debate—if debate is the right word for the endless exchange of platitudes—over whether it might not be better to read about foreign countries without the risk and expense of actually leaving home. It was of course in the interest of travel writers to argue that it was, that others should profit from their pains.

Travel had become a full-fledged and internationally recognized problem, and it received a full-fledged treatment at the hands of a German pedant named Jerome Turler (*De Peregrinatione, et Agro Neapolitano Libri II*, 1574; translated as *The Traveller*, 1575), who

> handled that argument according to the definitiue Methode, as they speake in
> the schooles; and haue comprehended also, as I iudge, in one Booke, what
> soeuer is necessarie for any to know concerning the due taking in hand of
> traueill, and the prosperous perfourming of the same. ["The Authors Pref-
> ace"]

This book is not fun to read, but it is thoroughly representative. Turler is beset
by the full range of anxieties, prejudices, and phobias; what he can say in
defense of travel makes it a narrow and strictly utilitarian undertaking. There
are two kinds of travel, one undertaken with an end in view; the other is
idleness. True travel

> is nothing else but a paine taking to see and searche forreine landes, not to
> bee taken in hand by all sorts of persons, or vnaduisedly, but such as are
> meete thereto, eyther to the ende that they may attayne to such artes and
> knowledge as they are desirous to learne or exercise: or else to see, learne,
> and diligently to marke suche things in strange Countries, as they shall haue
> neede to vse in the common trade of lyfe, whereby they maye profite them-
> selues, their friendes, and Countrey if neede require. [P. 5]

To justify the expense and danger, to keep out of trouble, and to prove he was
not wasting his time, the traveler was kept very busy with a course of self-
improvement. Turler gives instructions on how to describe a country, how to
produce a stereotype of each nationality, and so on. The second part of his
book is a description of Naples, a practical example to be imitated.

This literature of advice brought a new travel literature into being—the first
injunction was always to keep a journal—and provided a recipe for it. There are
all kinds of materials that Sandys inserts without any introduction, because
they were expected in a travel book. But he does more than excel in a genre
staked out by the likes of Jerome Turler. Sandys is one of a handful of men, all
roughly of the same generation, who have been called "urbane travellers."[13]
The urbane traveler is defined by his intentions: "a man of culture who was
touring Europe to complete his education, or to satisfy his spirit of curiosity, or
occasionally just to seek notoriety."[14] To travel with no more practical reason
than these was something new. It also put these men in a new relation to the
literature of travel.

Hakluyt's search for authors, for men with responsible identities, implicitly
contained an invitation for authors to establish literary identities. Sandys and
the three travellers who best bear comparison with him—Thomas Coryat,
William Lithgow, and Sir Henry Blount—are all literary performers. They
have internalized Hakluyt's canons of responsibility, but they also offer us the
spectacle of strong personalities (and sometimes intellects) in motion. And they
are literary men, each in his own way; they are responsible to a general cultural
tradition as well as to scientific standards of observation. They unite, each in

his own way, and none so ambitiously as Sandys, travel literature with literary culture.

All are travelers in Europe and the Mediterranean world, where their urbanity can be given full play.[15] Urbanity, and especially historical awareness, had become almost indispensable.

The logbook style of John Locke (1553; in Hakluyt, V, pp. 76–104) would be fine if he were coasting Newfoundland, but as he sails around Greece it only displays his ignorance. The reader did not want to hear that he passed Cephalonia in the morning, but that Odysseus lived nearby. Locke and men like him have to deliver their account simply, with no commentary except of the most formulaic kind on the significance of what they see. They were in no position to deliver a commentary, since they lacked the education in the classics on which nearly every kind of Renaissance commentary was based. Once a classical education could be assumed in the reader, it was the obvious way of orienting a description of the Mediterranean world.

Coryats Crudities (1611) was prefaced by a hundred pages of mock encomiums by his literary friends from Donne and Jonson on down. Coryat was a Cambridge M.A., but made his reputation as a buffoon: his five-month walking tour of Europe was a kind of stunt, as was the publication of the book about it. But Coryat was aware of a learned European travel literature, and it terrified him. He admits to having used Latin books he found in Italy to enlarge his descriptions; he intends to translate his own book into Latin as soon as he has time; again and again he refers to "travellers of that learning, that I am not worthy to loose their shoe-lachet" (p. 15). He demonstrates his own learning often enough—he collects inscriptions, visits Isaac Casaubon in Paris, and quotes classical poetry at appropriate moments—but we are left with the impression that his humanism is less a way of knowing about the classical world, as it is for Sandys, than another kind of performance. So he goes to Troy and has himself knighted there, and composes an *extempore* Latin oration.

William Lithgow also made a pilgrimage to Troy, in whose ruins we see him standing, dressed à la Turk, on the title page of *The Totall Discourse, of the Rare Aduentures, and painefull Peregrinations of long nineteen Yeares Trauayles, from Scotland, to the most Famous Kingdomes in Europe, Asia, and Affrica* (1632). The experience inspired him to compose a poem to Helen; "Borne to the Muses, as to the World, a mungrell to both," he is given to breaking into bad verse, often stuffed with classical mythology. His derisive humor, scurrilous invective, and aggressive lowbrow appropriation of history and literature are reminiscent of Nashe's *Unfortunate Traveller,* as is the picaresque pacing of his adventures.

If Lithgow is, stylistically at least, a lowbrow version of Sandys, Sir Henry Blount is in every way his antithesis. Blount's *Voyage into the Levant* (1636) is also the only English Renaissance travel book about the eastern Mediterranean whose interest is comparable to Sandys's *Relation.* Sandys was the orthodox son of an Archbishop; Blount was thought to have formed the thinking of his son Charles, the Deist. Sandys was nothing if not learned, the achievement of his book being based on his ability to control and mobilize the accumulated literary resources of his culture; Blount had a reputation at Oxford (according to Anthony à Wood) as being extraordinarily intelligent but not especially learned, and the interest of his book is in its radicalism, its eagerness to jettison received ideas and think things over anew. If Sandys transforms the headings prepared for travellers into full rhetorical *topoi,* Blount is interested in the implications of ideas. Sandys's book is a great public restatement of the meaning of the eastern Mediterranean for his culture; Blount's is a private intellectual adventure, whose outcome is in question. His rusé and ironic view of cross-cultural relations, his attention to the diseases of knowledge, his reasoning from principles, his habit of relating everything to the human mind and its powers, often in connection with physiology and climatic influences, all look forward to the Enlightenment.

All four of these urbane travellers display a Renaissance sense of form. It is different in each of them—Sandys's is the most objective, with his historical depth and his painterly portraits of cities and landscapes; the others' are more functions of their personalities—but in all cases it is in marked contrast to the formless accumulation of detail characteristic of medieval travellers. For the medievals—as for Pliny[16]—the significance of the foreign is simply its variety, so simple accumulation tends to be its method, and the list its typical rhetorical form. When Sandys includes a list it is for a direct and conscious rhetorical effect, or for a specific purpose (like listing trade goods). His forms, his formality, are literary, historical, rhetorical—in a word, humanist. What distinguishes his book is its willingness to take responsibility for itself as a free-standing artistic representation of the places he visited.

As his biographer has shown, Sandys was familiar with the sophisticated travel accounts, chorographical surveys and guide books being published on the Continent in Latin, Italian, and French.[17] Often he follows them closely, though finally his own book is probably more ambitious than any of his models in its historical and geographical sweep, and perhaps also in its thematic shaping. The point to be made here is that he was essentially the first to translate this learned tradition into English, creating a precedent that would be followed later by men like Sir Thomas Herbert, James Howell, and John Evelyn.

A note on Blount's life in Philip Bliss's edition of Wood's *Athenae Oxonesis* (1813) tells us that "merely on the merit of this book, he was appointed one of the band of pensioners" of Charles I (p. 54), which reminds us of the social and hence generic context of the works of our urbane travellers. Young gentlemen were regularly shipped off in the train of ambassadors or with voyages of discovery. They should be distinguished from the trained scientific observers— the young gentlemen had no discernible function. But they had read the literature of advice for travelers, and kept a journal, and when they returned this journal was circulated. Often it was their first public performance. If it was good enough it could be used to advertise their parts and education, and might lead to employment. Sandys's work can be seen in this light: it is the most impressive of these works (it was composed at a relatively advanced age), and served as a model for others.[18] (Sir Thomas Herbert's debt is obvious even from the title of his *Relation of Some Yeares Travaile, Begunne Anno 1626* [1634].) The significant point about this literature is that it requires the author both to prove himself as a responsible observer and to show his grip on his own culture, his cultivation, and to combine both elements with style and (if possible) *sprezzatura*. This literature is generically about the author and what he can say; it encourages amplitude and diversity of interests. Some literary talent is indispensable.

Sandys, Coryat, and Lithgow found an editor who could appreciate their literary skill in Samuel Purchas, whose *Hakluytus Posthumous, or Purchas his Pilgrimes* appeared in 1625. It is a massive compilation, twenty volumes in the Hakluyt Society reprint (1905). If Hakluyt's metaphor is the court, Purchas's is the theater:

> Lo here then (after my Pilgrimage of the former Nature, for such as like better that course) in open Theatre presented a Shew of Discoveries on an English stage, wherein the World is both the Spectacle and Spectator; the Actors are the Authors themselves, each presenting his owne actions and passions in that kind, kindly (in generous and genuine History) acting their acts; not affectedly straining, or scenic-all-ly playing their part; the Arts indeed of the Poet, Maker, or Composer, aiming at delight more than truth (Populo ut placerent, quas fecisset Fabulas) seeking to please the vulgar with fabulous wonders and wonder-foole fables.[19]

The theater is a dangerous metaphor, and Purchas has to emphasize that he, like Hakluyt, wants truthful, empirically based evidence: "I had rather heare the meanest of Ulysses his followers relating his wanderings, then wander from the certaintie with Homer after all his readings and conjectures." He finds that Sandys is too literary for his purposes—he cuts out all Sandys's poetic translations—but his admiration for the *Relation* and the affinity he feels with it are clear from his preface to his reprint of Sandys. This is, incidentally, as good criticism of the *Relation* as has been published to date.

> Like that Scribe which brings out of his Treasurie new and old; so have I here done, and so our Author following. To those elder Stories and Records I have added this later Voyage to Jerusalem and Constantinople: and He, besides his travels, hath added his Studies, the Voyage of his Minds Industrie, as well as of his bodies Peregrination; as a Learned Argus, seeing with the Eyes of many Authors, and comparing things old and new. Pardon me, that I have much pruned his sweet Poetrie, his farre-set Antiquitie, and other fruits of his Learning: I would not have his owne Worke out of request. I

present men rather as Travellers, then as Scholers; and in this Historicall Stage produce them, telling what they have seene; not what they can say, or what other Authors have written: not that I disprove this (for what else is my whole Pilgrimage?) but that I hold on here another course; where even brevitie it selfe is almost tedious (as you see) by Multitudes. The other parts of Master Sandys are not simply superfluous, yet are these to our present purpose sufficient.[20]

In spite of these reservations, Purchas's purposes are clearly literary. He always considers his reader and he cherishes his author/actors, instead of interrogating witnesses. He himself is the Master of Ceremonies in his world theater, intervening at will to keep the show moving, and irradiating the whole with his slightly demented rhetoric.

It is precisely his literary orientation that has made Purchas an embarrassment to a certain kind of historian. George Bruner Parks provides the most extreme and most scornful expression of a common position:

. . . Purchas was in no intelligible way concerned with the history and development of science or enterprise. . . . his purpose was naturally modeled by his interest; and that interest . . . was geographical and historical, to be sure; but the geography and history were of an amateurish, or one may say of a literary, sort.[21]

Parks is impatient with Purchas's tendency to contemplate and allegorize, and he is nauseated by the Brownean motion of his prose.

But the essential accusation in Parks's treatment of Purchas is that he "lacks dignity," which is Hakluyt's great virtue. Founding the Empire is great and solemn business, and everything connected with it should keep decorum. Certainly Hakluyt and Purchas are different in character. Hakluyt is Classic, virile, clear and noble; Purchas is Mannerist, extravagant, curious and fantastic in the Renaissance as well as modern senses of those words. Hakluyt was included in the ships' libraries of the first East Indiamen, enshrined from the start as the epic of imperialism; Purchas's most famous reader was an opium-intoxicated poet.

Most of what has ever been written about English Renaissance travel and geographical literature was produced in the 1920s and 1930s, in the wake of the great editorial projects of the Hakluyt Society. That literature offered the attraction of a good story coupled with the chance to celebrate the simultaneous rise of imperialism and empiricism, both then still in their heyday. From this perspective the more literary works appeared as deviations from the line of progress and scientific advancement.[22] So E. G. R. Taylor is as scornful towards Peter Heylyn as Parks is towards Purchas: "Heylyn's literary bent is seen to greater advantage in the closing sections of his work, where he finds space for Fairyland, Utopia, the Land of Chivalry, and the New World in the Moon."[23] Or R. W. Frantz, whose *The English Traveller and the Movement of Ideas*

1660–1732 is a celebration of the work of the Royal Society in suppressing the literary element in travel literature: "It would not be right, however, to overlook exceptions to the rule. In the main, they take the form of pedantry," he writes,[24] naming Sandys, Coryat, and Herbert as examples.

These historians are perpetuating the attitudes of the period just after Sandys, the attitudes most clearly expressed by the Royal Society, attitudes which would restructure the genre of travel writing. As the 17th century progressed travel literature broke up into several genres, each with its own well-defined norms—the scientific description, the adventure story, the antiquarian survey, and so on. The later instructions for travelers demanded natural history at the expense of attention to culture, hard empirical data rather than speculations about what a place might mean. But in the era before this generic differentation the travel writer was free to do it all. This was admittedly a confusing demand, and produced a lot of confused work; but it is a very interesting moment, and Sandys at least was capable of meeting the multifarious demands of the genre with the resources of the rich literary tradition of humanism.

2

The Literary Character of the *Relation*

It is already been said that the *Relation* is the most "literary" of English Renaissance travel books; the purpose of this chapter is to estimate what this means. The polish of its prose, the poetic translations with which it is studded, and the erudition with which it sometimes bristles are easy enough to notice, but they need to be understood as something more than a literary veneer, however attractive this is thought to be, let alone a layer of pedantry larded onto an original travel journal. It is the *Relation*'s full engagement with humanist learning that is most significant about it in literary historical terms, and for interpretative purposes it is crucial to understand how it participates in a literary system, and how the experiences of Sandys the traveler are related to the purposes of Sandys the writer.

The presence of other texts in Sandys's book does not simply serve to mediate his perceptions of the eastern Mediterranean, though it certainly does that in important ways; the other texts are inherent in his subject matter, *are* his subject matter. Traveling in the world and reading about it are inseparable activities. Michel Foucault has explained this as a characteristic of 16th century epistemology, speaking of "a non-distinction between what is seen and what is read, between observation and relation, which results in the constitution of a single, unbroken surface in which observation and language intersect to infinity." He continues, discussing the naturalist Aldrovandi:

> When one is faced with the task of writing an animal's *history*, it is useless and impossible to choose between the profession of naturalist and that of compiler: one has to collect together into one and the same form of knowledge all that has been *seen* and *heard*, all that has been *recounted*, either by nature or by men, by the language of the world, by tradition, or by the poets. To know an animal or a plant, or any terrestrial thing whatever, is to gather together the whole dense layer of signs with which it or they may have been covered . . .[1]

In general what places mean to Sandys is closely related to what they have always meant. Fame is as much his subject as a more factual history: his

40

dominant theme is the contrast between ancient fame and modern desolation. The poets and the historians are his natural allies in this project. So everything that has been written about the places he visits becomes part of his subject matter, as much so as the place itself. The poets are sources and conveyors of fame; they are also evidence of it. Sandys establishes that Sicily deserves the epithet "Queene of the *Mediterranean* islands" by piling up passages about it from famous authors, thereby simultaneously measuring and specifying the significance Sicily has for an educated European (pp. 234–35).

He will use the literary tradition associated with a place as the surest guide to its significance as long as such a tradition is available to him. His description of Naples, for instance, may owe an unacknowledged debt to an anonymous "Relatione di Napoli"[2] and perhaps to other such literature as well as to Statius and Virgil and the Neo-Latin poets who are quoted, but this reliance on a local tradition of writing about Naples was surely deliberate and nothing Sandys would have apologized for. He quotes a poem in which Statius describes the varieties of beautiful stone brought from all over the Greek world to adorn Naples, which might serve as a metaphor for the way the Naples he builds with words incorporates materials which are already beautiful and multicolored and polished. A Naples made out of prose and poetry already exists, and it is as much "there" for Sandys as the physical city. The literary Naples is an emana-tion of the city, spoken through its writers, a collectively elaborated re-creation that has the same history as the city itself. Sandys's Naples should be, as far as possible, a translation of this language whose relation with the city is intimate and long established, giving it an authority and authenticity, a correspondence of word and thing which could never be obtained by the invention of a single foreign observer. To be sure these materials are not so firmly organized that they do not permit Sandys to rearrange and select them to serve his own purposes, to mold them in the form required by his book, and the translation into English involves some transformations which are not merely linguistic; but there is no attempt to denature the sources. A note of native pride and enthusiasm about the city is carried over into Sandys's prose.

Occasionally the ancient reputation of a place absorbs Sandys's attention to the point that the modern site is altogether displaced from his account. For example nearly everything he has to say about Sinuessa (on the coast of Cam-pania) is concerned with a paradoxical opposition between health and deprav-ity, illustrated by several incidents from Roman history.

> These waters are said to cure women of their barrennesse, and men of their madnesse; but men rather here lose their wits with too much sensuality, as women that defect by the forfeiture of their vertues; sicknesse being but a pretence of their gadding: of old iested at by the *Epigrammatist* [Martial] . . . [P. 303]

He does not explore the claim that the waters are medicinal, nor is it clear the baths still exist—all we are told about what was there in 1611 is that "*Sinuessa* shewed us her relikes."

But Sandys's themes find their fullest expression when both terms, ancient reputation and modern desolation, are in play. The relation between them can be intricately developed, as in his description of the Roman pleasure resort of Baiae. The description of the ancient city is effected largely through passages from Horace, Martial, Seneca and Ovid, which are already concerned with its reputation.[3] Perhaps the most crucial one is from Horace, introduced as a transition (and a connection) between the account of its physical site and an evaluation of its emblematic moral significance.

> They forced the Sea to retire, and affoord a foundation for their sumptuous buildings. Scoft at in a certaine old man by the *Lyric:*
>
> > Thou marble putst to cut, thy end now neare,
> > And thoughtlesse of thy tombe, do'st houses reare:
> > Inforcing Baiae to vsurpe the bound
> > Of muttering seas; not pleasd with the dry ground.
> >
> > Hor. 1.2 Od. 18
>
> *AEgyptian Canopus,* mentioned before, was a schoole of vertue compared to the voluptuous liberty of this City. The Inne (saith *Seneca*) and receptable for vices . . . [P. 291]

In 1611 there is nothing left but some ruins.

> But behold an egregious example, that pronounceth the works of mens hands as fraile as the workmen. *Baiae,* not much inferiour vnto *Rome* in magnificency, equall in beautie, and superiour in healthfull situation, hath now scarce one stone left aboue another, demolished by warre, and deuoured by water. For it should seeme that the *Lombards* and *Saracens* in the destruction hereof had not onely a hand; but that the extruded sea hath againe regained his vsurped limits: made apparent by the paued streets, and traces of foundations to be seene vnder water. [P. 292]

Time has pointed the moral of the Horace poem; Sandys's transition to the modern ruins illustrates a process whose terms and even the images by which it is expressed had already been thoroughly prepared for him. Baiae is a kind of commonplace in the moral inheritance from antiquity, and that fact is more interesting and important than archaeological details about the site: the commonplace determines the way in which the place will be considered.

By no means all of the classical quotations and references carry so much thematic weight: the majority are inserted because they contain a relevant bit of information. Sandys committed himself in the dedication to describing the ancient as well as present states of the places he visited, and this could best be done out of ancient authors. The epics in particular are filled with various kinds of historical materials in which the Renaissance was very much interested: genealogies, stories about the foundations of cities and kingdoms, migrations, customs, and so on. They could still be taken seriously as the authoritative compendia of the arts and sciences of their civilizations.

Seriously, but not uncritically—there are passages crowded with ancient authorities who have lost their authority. A story about a friendly dolphin leads Sandys to compile all the dolphin lore he can find, but one gets the impression that he is playing with his library in a mood of amused scepticism:

> But beleeue who that will, the story of the Dolphin frequenting this Lake, reported by *Plinie* vpon the testimony of *Maecenas, Flauianus,* and *Flauius Alsius,* who insert it in their chronicles; . . . *Appian* both witnesse as much: and *Solinus . . . Pausanias* doth report himself to haue bene an eye witnesse almost of the like. And *Pliny.* . . . If these be true, why may we not credite the story of *Arion* the musitian . . . related by *Herodotus* and others? But because I thinke it a fable, I will rather choose the report of a Poet [Ovid] . . . [Pp. 276–77]

The authority of the ancients assures that their opinion will be heard, but Sandys does not feel compelled to agree with them. This does not always advance our understanding of the object under scrutiny. Sandys's procedure in this passage and others is critical, but it does not lead to the truth—the process of inquiry ends when the sources give out. He is not committed to the truth of any one particular text, but he is committed to basing his intellectual life in a body of texts; knowledge is organized as the accretion of commentaries, a system in which the original text is never thrown away. Sandys's later master-piece is a compendium of the Renaissance arts and sciences arranged as a commentary on Ovid—a massive illustration of this habit of mind.

Within such a system criticism of sources is necessary in order to keep ancient errors from being endlessly reproduced. Verification of inherited descriptions of the places he visited was certainly one of Sandys's major purposes. Normally it is the ancients who are used to further Sandys's descriptive purposes, but sometimes the balance is reversed and an independent interest in producing footnotes to the ancient authors emerges: the reason for visiting Troy is in order to be able to write a topographical commentary on Homer and Virgil. Here too Sandys was following his readers' interests: a great deal of what the terrain meant to them arose from its associations with the familiar classics.

There is also a handful of references and quotations that are likely to strike a modern reader as perfectly irrelevant. They are mostly the result of Sandys's habit of deriving whatever he can from a classical source. This was, of course, a habit Sandys shared with other humanists, and it usually stands him in good stead. But it occasionally results in pseudo-derivations like the following, about the Moors in Acre:

> Here wrastle they in breeches of oyled leather, close to their thighs: their bodies naked and annointed according to the ancient vse, deriued, as it should seeme by *Virgil,* from the *Trojans;*

> Disrob'd they wrastle in their countries guise
> With gliding oyle ———— [p. 205]

This peculiar use of "according to" was common among Sandys's contemporaries: it means "corresponding to", though it suggests something more. "Derived" can refer to nothing but "the ancient use," and Sandys knows it, but he clearly wishes it were otherwise and the grammar comes perilously close to fulfilling his desires at the expense of historical accuracy. Sandys's mind contained an enormous archive of erudite information such as this, and sometimes he succumbs to the temptation to make connections within the archive, though he cannot relate them historically to anything he sees. Similarly, he occasionally seems to imply knowledge of the classics in people (like the Turks) who cannot have known them:

> With the *Stoicks* they attribute all accidentes to destinie, and constellations at birth, and say with the *Tragedian* [Seneca],
>
> Fates guide us . . . [P. 57]

If a foreigner expresses a belief similar to one which has received canonical expression in the western tradition, the two will be coupled rather unscrupulously and, we may feel, gratuitously. In this too Sandys was following a venerable tradition: one remembers Mandeville's Far Eastern polygamists quoting (in Latin) the Biblical injunction to multiply and subdue the earth. One might undertake a defense of such illogical conjunctions of the ancient and the foreign on the grounds that knowledge of the ancient world, which was held in common by the learned of Europe, contained the largest body of ethnological data the Renaissance had; references to it might constitute an attempt to establish rudimentary categories by which data could be organized and assimilated in the absence of more abstract categories. It might also be said that any attempt by a Renaissance writer to establish a continuity of moral life between himself and a foreigner should be applauded. Using classical intermediaries also created problems, but if it helped, so much the better. The hermeneutical consequences of Sandys's classicizing habit will be examined in more detail in Part II.

While the ancient poets and historians are proudly displayed on the surface of the text, acknowledgment of contemporary sources is minimal, erratic, and often misleading. (Other travelers are usually mentioned only when they stand in need of correction.) The attentive reader may, for instance, be disconcerted to notice that Sandys sails by Cyprus and Crete without going ashore, although he inserts full descriptions of both islands (pp. 218–25) which are almost indistinguishable from his normal manner. E. S. de Beer has written a short study of a section of Book 4 showing in some detail how Sandys used his sources for this passage; showing, in fact, that the passage is almost entirely a compilation from four Italian sources.[4] Sandys's appropriation of these sources is thorough and critical; he takes over small units, often smaller than a sentence, rearranging them and using them to construct his own patterns and carry his own themes.

These sections of the *Relation* are not at all typical of the whole book, but they are revealing of the extent to which the literary tradition could become self-sustaining and self-enclosing. Admittedly, source studies is a cruel science when directed at travel literature, at least as long as one believes that romance and novelty and authenticity are at the heart of the genre. Sandys's procedures will not surprise anyone familiar with the ways of Renaissance travel writers, for whom outright plagiarism and "personal" accounts of places where they had never been were standard. Sandys is actually quite scrupulous about both matters: one can always tell whether he did or did not go to the place he is describing, though he may not emphasize the distinction, and he always re-works his materials. But source studies will help us to locate Sandys's intentions and originality. He was interested in being accurate, critical and useful, rather than romantic and novel, and used authenticity to buttress his authoritativeness rather than as an end in itself.

Although the *Relation* is loosely organized around Sandys's itinerary, the narrative of his personal experiences has to compete with other forms of narration which are often of greater structural importance; no meanings as important as those connected with the public moral and historical theme of "threatening instructions" are generated around these personal experiences.

There is a complete lack of personal reflection in Sandys's *Relation*. This is doubtless partly the result of his disinterest in writing about himself. Shortly before his death he wrote one of his very few original poems, "Deo Opt. Max.," of which the second part is a brief autobiography.

> O who hath tasted of Thy clemency
> In greater measure or more oft than I!
> My grateful verse Thy goodness shall display,
> O Thou, Who went'st along in all my way,
> To where the morning with perfumed wings
> From the high mountains of Panchaea springs;
> To that new-found-out world, where sober night
> Takes from the antipodes her silent flight;
> To those dark seas, where horrid winter reigns,
> And binds the stubborn floods in icy chains;
> To Lybian wastes, whose thirst no show'rs assuage,
> And where swoll'n Nilus cools the lion's rage.
> Thy wonders in the deep have I beheld,
> Yet all by those on Judah's hills excell'd:
> There where the Virgin's Son His doctrine taught,
> His miracles, and our redemption wrought:
> Where I, by Thee inspir'd, His praises sung,
> And on His Sepulchre my off'ring hung.

Which way soe'er I turn my face or feet,
I see Thy glory, and Thy mercy meet.[5]

This passage is utterly characteristic of Sandys: his own life is presented as a commentary on God's mercies; his travels to the four corners of the world (a classical world, which still had corners) frame a central Christian experience at the center of the Christian world. His piety combines with his breadth of experience and learning to transform his life into a pattern, expressed in traditional terms, which carries a religious meaning. The personal element has largely disappeared into this pattern.

In the *Relation* these same experiences are not organized into any such pattern, even one so self-effacing as this. This is not to say that we do not hear about Sandys's adventures, or that each page is not permeated with his personality and his critical presence. But his trip as such, as a series of personal experiences, is not given a significant form: there is no psychological development, no religious allegory (e.g. of pilgrimage), no deepening of knowledge or poetic impressions. The world Sandys travels through is full of symbolic patterns (and these patterns are the real subject of his book) but they are not attached to his life or (except occasionally) to his passage through the landscape in which they are involved.

The element of personal narrative is so attenuated and intermittent that several conflicting conventions can be used to govern it without producing an effect of incongruity. Sandys calls his book a "Iournall" on page 1 and at various other points—doubtless he kept a journal on which he based the *Relation*. He refers to "this year 1610" (p. 73), the year of the trip, not of the book, and there are occasional signs of spontaneous composition ("but I had almost forgot the Nestorians," p. 173), but there is no attempt to present the book as something written up each night. On a few rare occasions he sets up his narration in a day-to-day pattern clearly based on the journal (e.g. as he rows around Sicily), but on the whole the journal form is not adhered to. This greatly reduces the quantity of day-to-day detail given about his trip; it also keeps his book from being clogged with the mechanical recording of movements, as so many travel accounts are. At other times he seems to be reconstructing his account from memory ("as I remember," "if I forget not"); at others he adopts a guide book style, sometimes taking it over from his source ("you are about to descend," "Before we go to Putzole").

Against these passages should be set some which could only have been written in a library—the discussion of the flooding of the Nile, with its crowd of learned authorities, or the pages filled with lengthy quotations from the poets. He does not introduce these quotations as lines he thought of as he stood in front of whatever is being described, although he must often have done so.[6] We often follow his mind through patterns of association, but they are those of a scholar in a good library rather than those of an enraptured traveller.

Sandys's predominant rhetorical stance, then, locates him in a library rather than on the road. A great deal of the *Relation* could have been written without leaving England, whereas an account of his trip itself without learning acquired elsewhere would be an unrecognizably different work. As it is the narrative regularly lapses, sometimes for a very long time, while Sandys inserts a description of the place in which he had just arrived, in the manner of Herodotus's accounts of Egypt and Scythia. Or on a smaller scale, Sandys reduces the experiences he had while locked inside the Temple of the Sepulcher in Jerusalem during three days of Holy Week—which must have been chaotic and overwhelming—to an orderly description of the building (following the floor plan, not the order in which he saw it), and a series of ethnologies of the various exotic Christian sects (pp. 160–73).

Sometimes the descriptions are more closely linked to Sandys's experiences than this, but it is scarcely an exaggeration to say that the structural role of the trip and the narrative of it functions chiefly as a means of moving from one place (with its description) to another, and that their importance is reduced, often to nothing, once he arrives. The journal/relation form as he uses it performs this minimal task efficiently, and it makes no further demands on him, though it permits him to insert material arranged with a great deal of formal artistry. It does not force him to give his own experiences any form, and in fact the book as a whole, and the individual books within it, dribble away to disappointingly inconclusive endings. The breakdown of literary form at these points is in striking contrast to the high finish of most of the book, and indicates that Sandys's artistic attention was directed towards the things he saw rather than towards himself as an observer, a matter which seemed not to be in need of discussion.

The traveler in this book is a serious man seeking public meanings through history, allegories, an antique and monumental literary tradition, and so on—he has not equipped himself to observe the accidents and random delicacies of life. Without generic conventions demanding its inclusion, each incident would have to justify its presence in the *Relation*. It is important to remember that many of the novelistic conventions and techniques with which later travelers give form—and therefore significance—to their experiences had not yet been invented, so that those experiences might pass with no literary record. The result is perhaps less detail than we would like, but on the other hand all the anecdotes Sandys gives us have overcome the lack of supporting conventions and are quite good. If his travel experiences are not of continuous structural importance as the containing form of the contents of the *Relation*, they are by no means ignored.

Here is an especially fine example, which blossoms as unexpectedly in the text as it did in Sandys's experience. He refuses to leave Malta with his ship:

> But no intreatie could get me aboord; choosing rather to vndergo all hazards and hardnesse whatsoeuer, then so long a voyage by sea, to my nature so irksome. And so was I left alone on a naked promentorie right

against the Citie, remote from the concourse of people, without prouision, and not knowing how to dispose of my selfe. At length a little boate made towards me, rowed by an officer appointed to attend on strangers that had not Pratticke, lest others by coming into their companie should receiue the infection: who carried me to the hollow hanging of a rocke, where I was for that night to take vp my lodging; and the day following to be conueyed by him vnto the *Lazaretta,* there to remaine for thirtie or fortie daies before I could be admitted into the Citie. But behold an accident, which I rather thought at first to haue bene a vision, then (as I found it) reall. My guardian being departed to fetch me some victuals, laid along, and musing on my present condition, a *Phalucco* arriueth at the place. Out of which there stept two old women; the one made me doubt whether she were so or no, she drew her face into so many formes, and with such anticke gestures stared vpon me. These two did spread a *Turkie* carpet on the rocke, and on that a table-cloth, which they furnished with varietie of the choisest viands. Anon another arriued, which set a Gallant ashore with his two *Amarosaes,* attired like Nymphs, with lutes in their hands, full of disport and sorcery. For little would they suffer him to eate, but what he receiued with his mouth from their fingers. Sometimes the one would play on the lute whilest the other sang, and laid his head in her lap; their false eies looking vpon him, as if their hearts were troubled with passions. The attending hags had no small part in the comedie, adminstring matter of mirth with their ridiculous moppings. Who indeed (as I after heard) were their mothers; borne in *Greece,* and by them brought hither to trade amongst the vnmarried fraternitie. At length the *French* Captaine (for such he was, and of much regard) came and in-treated me to take a part of their banquet; which my stomacke perswaded me to accept of. He willed them to make much of the *Forestier:* but they were not to be taught entertainment; and grew so familiar, as was to neither of our likings. But both he and they, in pitie of my hard lodging, did offer to bring me into the Citie by night (an offence, that if knowne, is punished by death,) and backe againe in the morning. Whilest they were vrging me thereunto, my guardian returned; with him a *Maltese,* whose father was an English man: he made acquainted therewith, did by all meanes dehort them. At length (the Captaine hauing promised to labour my admittance into the Citie) they departed. When a good way from shore, the curtizans stript themselues, and leapt into the sea; where they violated all the prescriptions of modestie. But the Captaine the next morning was not vndmindfull of his promise; soliciting the Great Maister in my behalfe, as he sate in councel; who with the assent of the great Crosses, granted me Pratticke. So I came into the Citie, and was kindly entertained in the house of the aforesaid *Maltese;* where for three weekes space, with much contentment I remained. [P. 227]

This episode justifies itself as it is directly concerned with the basic plot of Sandys's travels—but he has clearly seen, and taken, the opportunity to "make something of" it. He makes a literary anecdote, loosely based on literary conventions. At the beginning of this paragraph we get an unprecedented amount of attention to Sandys's personal situation and state of mind. He has suddenly become a fictional character, the kind of forlorn pastoral solitary to whom visions occur. The unreality of this "vision" and its vaguely literary resonances allow Sandys to fictionalize it in the heightened terms of a Romance adventure ("full of disport and sorcery"). He is of course greatly aided in this project by the theatricality of the participants ("attired like Nymphs"). This adventure and the terms with which to express it are thrust upon him, and he accepts them; but it should also be clear how unByronic Sandys is. He is not given to romanticizing his experiences. Nor does he allegorize them (although this episode clearly establishes Guyon as Sandys's great original). Any Renaissance traveler was by an inevitable convention an Odysseus, but few encountered such palpable incarnations of the Homeric temptresses—it is probably to Sandys's credit that he avoided an easy allusion, and this too is typical of him. The proximity of the Romance conventions allows the narrative to burst into unusual fictional vividness for a moment, but Sandys restrains the invocation of a model which would overburden the situation and imply a continued allegory which does not exist. The effect of this anecdote is strictly local and self-contained.

Other incidents with less literary flavor serve to convey local color and national character; another sort of personal experience is described because it will be relevant to other travellers. The *Relation* is not primarily intended as a travel guide, but it does contain a considerable amount of information on subjects such as methods of transportation, tariffs, and especially dangerous passages. These and other incidents are related to the conditions (political, historical, economic, military, and so on) which gave rise to them. Sandys is very attentive to the web of such forces through which he moves, and when they affect his movement he uses the occasion to talk about them. The concrete immediacy of these incidents supplements the more extended and formal descriptions of institutions and historical events.

Passing remarks about the conditions of travel can be very poignant. Sandys gets his Greek sailors to put him ashore at Troy only "with much importunitie and promise of reward (it being a matter of danger)" (p. 19). The fear of pirates keeps Sandys from exploring the whole site: he has to content himself with a view of the plain from the Promontory of Sigeum. This means he must rely on Pierre Belon for a description of the ruins of Ilium (p. 22), although from where he stands he can tell that Belon has poorly described the rivers on the plain, and he will later express his contempt for Belon's powers of observation in the only other reference to him (on p. 31). Of course an accurate description of the site would require the techniques of modern archaeology, but we see here a serious attempt to apply careful classical scholarship and some archaeological sophistication, an attempt which is thwarted by conditions rendering it impossible for the observer to approach the object of his study. The implications of this are important for the form and quality of European scholarship: the East (and parts of Europe as well) was not accessible as it would be later during Western imperialist domination of the region.[7]

In 1610 piracy in the Mediterranean was at its height (Elizabeth's now unem-
ployed sea-dogs bing not the least of the problem), the political and military
situation in the Lebanon was as usual chaotic and dangerous, the deserts of
Arabia, Egypt and Palestine were inhabited by Bedouin who made their living
by robbery and extortion, Palestine was further beset by lawless troops connected with the fighting against the Persians in Syria, the Sicilians were so
hostile that travel in the interior was impossible except for large well-armed
bands (Sandys cannot climb Mt. Aetna because "the countrey hereabout is
daily foraged by theeues," p. 242), and in Calabria "Ouer-land there is no
trauelling without assured pillage, and hardly to be auoided murder" (p. 250).
So the story goes—it is too familiar to the 17th century traveler to call for much
comment. The traveler could not wander freely over the landscape: he was
almost always confined to the network (ship, embassy, caravan) which assured
him a tolerable degree of safety. Understandably, his narrative was also
confined to a well-beaten path.

Sandys the traveler often seems like a fugitive, with only a distant and
precarious view of sights too dangerous to approach; this is in contrast to the
assured sense of familiarity and possession with respect to the same landscape
which emanates from the poets and historians of Imperial Rome. The rising
cultural power of the Renaissance had reduced these authors to a province of
learning, but it had not yet attacked the East politically. So it tended to base its
descriptions on these sources which were in its domain, subject to established
critical methods, and available for leisurely contemplation, rather than on the
actuality which was not subdued by teams of surveyors, anthropologists, travel
writers or painters, and the military and political power which made this
invasion possible.

The fugitive quality of Sandys's travels is not something he dwells on: we
usually discover it only because he is (as has been said) unusually scrupulous
about telling us exactly what he has seen with his own eyes. He supplies the
deficiencies of his own observation fully and for the most part silently out of
ancient or, when necessary, modern authors. The contrast between his experiences and the collective store of knowledge on which he draws is usually
disguised rather than developed. One of the more remarkable exceptions to this
is the description of his ride around Mount Carmel, and it is very much to the
point here, because his experience was determined by the political situation—
the situation in Palestine as a whole, and in the tourist network in particular.
Sandys had contracted with a *Muccermen* (muleteer) to take him to Acre, much
to the anger of a Greek named Atala whom Sandys had already mentioned as
rapaciously abusing his monopoly on the conveyance of pilgrims between
Jerusalem and the ports. Eight miles beyond Rama

> . . . the *Muccermen* would haue stayd (which we would not suffer being then
> the best time of the day for trauell) that they might by night haue auoided the
> next village, with the paiments there due: where we were hardly intreated by

the procurement of *Attala,* who holds correspondency with *Moores* of those quarters. They would not take lesse than foure dollars a man (when perhaps as many Medeins were but due) and that with much iangling. They sought occasion how to trouble vs; beating vs off our Mules, because forsooth we did not light to do homage to a sort of halfe-clad rascals; pulling the white Shash from the head of the *Portugall* (whereby he well hoped to haue past for a *Turke*) his Iannizary looking on. Here detained they vs vntil two of the clock the next morning, without meate, without sleepe, couched on the wet earth, and washed with raine; yet expecting worse, and then suffered vs to depart. After a while we entred a goodly forest, full of tall and delightful trees, intermixed with fruitfull and flowery launes. Perhaps the earth affoordeth not the like; it cannot a more pleasant. Hauing passed this part of the wood (the rest inclining to the West, and then againe extending to the North) we might discouer a number of stragling tents, some iust in our way, and neare to the skirts of the forrest. These were *Spaheis* belonging to the hoast of *Morat Bassa,* then in the confines of *Persia.* They will take (especially from a Christian) whatsoeuer they like; and kindly they vse him if he passe without blowes: nor are their Commanders at all times free from their insolencies. To auoid them, we strucke out of the way, and crossed the pregnant champion to the foot of the mountaines, where for that day we reposed our selues: when it grew dark, we arose, inclining on the left hand, mingling after a while with a small Caruan of Moores; enioyned to silence, and to ride without our hats, lest discouered for Christians. The clouds fell down in streames, and the pitchie night had bereft vs of the conduct of our eyes, had not the lightning affoorded a terrible light. And when the raine intermitted, the aire appeared as if full of sparkles of fire, borne to and fro with the wind, by reason of the infinite swarmes of flies that do shine like glow-wormes, to a stranger a strange spectacle. In the next wood we out-stript that Caruan, where the theeuish *Arabs* had made sundry fires; to which our footmen drew neare to listen, that we might passe more securely. An houre after midnight the skie began to cleare, when on the other side of the wood we fell amongst certain tents of *Spaheis;* by whom we past with as little noise as we could, secured by their sounder sleepings. Not farre be-yond, through a large glade, betweene two hills, we leisurely descended for the space of two houres (a torrent rushing down on the left hand of vs) when not able longer to keepe the backes of our mules, we laid vs downe in the bottome vnder a plump of trees on the far side of a torrent. With the Sunne we arose, and found our selues at the East end, and North side of mount *Carmel.* [Pp. 202–3]

The moment Sandys relocates himself northeast of Mount Carmel he can re-sume his more normal style. The ability to name the mountain restores his access to all the accumulated knowledge about it: he can provide a perspica-cious general description of it, can quote Suetonius on the oracle of the god Carmelus, can give a brief history of the Carmelite Friars. The sentences regain the pomp and complexity appropriate to their freight of history and historical sensibility:

Ten miles South of this, stood that famous *Caesarea* (more anciently called the Tower of *Strato,* of a King of *Aradus* the builder so named who liued in the dayes of *Alexander*) in such sort reedified by *Herod,* that it little declined in magnificency from the principall cities of *Asia;* now leuell with the floore, the hauen lost, and situation abandoned. [P. 203]

It does not matter that Sandys did not see this site—the paragraph about Mount Carmel which this sentence concludes contains no reference to the traveler George Sandys.

But in the earlier passage the pressures of a hostile environment interrupt Sandys's leisurely ride past the antiquities of the Holy Land, physically assaulting him and threatening worse, forcing him to be literally a fugitive. As a result the landscape draws more closely around the traveler, losing its names and its history, translating itself into a series of intense experiences. These experiences are of wildly different kinds—fear, discomfort, wonder at natural beauty, the thrill of adventures in the dark, exhaustion—and the series is as haphazard as it is hazardous. He is wandering in a dark wood with no transcendent allegory to order the sequence. Here if anywhere Sandys feels the traveler's exaltation when his experiences reach the intensity of poetry, but the mystery of the experience is left unexplicated; the exotic flavor of the passage depends on the events themselves. Sandys's prose becomes more detailed to compensate for the lost ability to generalize, to be objective and historical, but remains very simple and unobtrusive. One does not have the impression that the episode is being developed through a conscious literary style, or that Sandys had a style prepared that would do the job. The techniques he uses could not be used to impart atmosphere to a situation less full of interest.

One more long passage may be quoted to illustrate this fact—that some of the more extraordinary of his personal experiences are expressed through a breakdown of his consciously literary style, and not through some set of devices especially elaborated to deal with them. The end of Book 3 brings Sandys to Acre, where he takes ship for England, bringing the Oriental section of his travels to a close. In striking contrast to the opening of Book 4, which is the rhetorical high point of the *Relation,* Book 3 concludes with a chaotic influx of undigested material.

The next morning after two or three houres riding, we ascended the mountaines of *Saron,* high and woody; which stretch with intermitted valleys, vnto the sea of Galily; and here haue their white cliffes washt with the surges; called *Capo Bianco* by the mariner: frequented (though forsaken by men) with Leopards, Bores, Iaccalls, and such like sauage inhabitants. This passage is both dangerous and difficult, neighboured by the precipitating cliffe, and made by the labour of man: yet recompensing the trouble with fragrant sauours, bayes, rosemary, marioram, hysope, and the like there growing in abundance. They say, that of late a theefe pursued on all sides, and desperate of his safety, (for rarely are offences here pardoned) leapt from the top into the Sea, and swum vnto *Tyrus,* which is seuen miles distant; who for the strangenesse of the fact was forgiuen by the *Emer.* A little beyond we passed by a ruinous fort, called *Scandarone* of *Alexander* the builder; here built to defend this passage: much of the foundation ouergrowne with osiers and weedes, being nourished by a Spring that falleth from thence into the Sea. A *Moore* not long since was here assailed by a Leopard, that sculkt in the aforesaid thicket; and iumping vpon him, ouerthrew him from his asse: but the beast hauing wet his feete, and mist of his hold, retired as ashamed without further violence. Within a day or two after he drew company together to haue hunted him, but found him dead of a wound receiued from a Bore. The higher mountaines now coming short of the Sea, do leaue a narrow leuell betweene. Vpon the left hand on a high round hill, we saw two solitary pillars, to which some of vs rid, in hope to have seene something of antiquitie; where we found diuers others laid along, with the halfe buried foundation of an ample building. A mile beyond we came to a fort maintained by a small garrison of *Moores,* to prohibit that passage if need should require, and to secure the traueller from theeues; a place heretofore vnpassable by reason of their out-rages. The souldiers acquainted with our merchants, freely entertained vs, and made vs good cheare according to their manner of diet: requited with a present of a little Tobacco, by them greedily affected. They also remitted our Caphar, vsing to take foure dollars apeece of the stranger Christians. From hence ascending the more eminent part of the rocky and naked mountaines, which here again thrust into the Sea, (called in times past the *Tyrian* ladder) by a long and steepe descent we descended into the valley of *Acre.* Diuerse little hills beeing here and there dispersed, crowned with ruines (the couerts for theeues) and many villages on the skirts of the bordering mountaines. Eare yet night, we reentred *Acre.* [P. 217]

Sandys's usual formality gives way here, allowing us to see the raw materials on which he works (one imagines that the original journal read much like this). In this surrender to the haphazardousness of experience, this temporary uncertainty about the standards which determine what is to be included and excluded, this lack of coherence and order, Sandys resembles his medieval predecessors and his unlettered contemporaries—or even a learned figure like Belon who had no sense of literary form. Low-grade marvels and random descriptions are allowed to claim his attention, which is usually restricted to more consequential matters.

It should be noted that the breakdown is not really one of stylistic surface, though the amount of attention given to style perhaps declines after the first sentences. Nor is a rapid sequence of powerful experiences responsible (as in the Mount Carmel episode) for the jumbled effect of this passage. The jumble is on another level, an epistemological one. There is a good deal of information here, historical and miscellaneous, but its lack of organization makes it seem random. One can feel Sandys groping towards the patterns which were basic to his mind (and typical of his culture): patterns of historical decline and displacement, of compensation, of appropriateness, of unique human achievement.

The stories about the Leopard point to a nature which for Sandys is full of moral meaning, of wonderful balances and hidden correspondences, but in this case he seems not to know what they mean. The patterns do not articulate the facts with enough clarity to be intelligible or to shape them into an encompassing form.

We see Sandys ride off the track "in hope to haue seene something of antiquitie," but the ruins remain unnamed for once, and therefore mysterious. As a movement toward historical identification, toward the terms which dominate the *Relation*, it is thwarted and produces no antiquarian interest; but its very inconclusiveness and mysteriousness capture an aspect of travel which, as I have been saying, Sandys does not dwell on and perhaps had no vocabulary to express. Likewise the rather acute rendering of the landscape coupled with arrested movements toward intelligible patterning might be taken as an expression of his final experiences in the Levant. How deliberate this expression is would be very difficult to say. It might be claimed that Sandys has simply become careless for a moment, that the disorganization is meaningless, and that to claim anything more is to overread. But one can perhaps still say that the generic complexity (or confusion) of this work contains a recognition that personal experience goes on after and between the large structures (the formal descriptions of countries and the political/historical/etc. reality they express) which organize life and meaning, especially public meanings of the kind Sandys is concerned with; that although these edifices of organized perception may swallow up the individual for long periods at a time, he is left with a residue of materials and experiences which seem to demand some kind of expression. Perhaps he was simply confused by this demand; certainly it is too much to claim that he used it to liberate himself from the very strict if complex definitions and patterns he had imposed on the Levant; but it is here, in this temporary release from them, that we may look for a gesture toward including kinds of meanings which he does not develop, based on a more generous and personal attitude towards the various and chaotic nature of the traveler's experience.

The negligence with which Sandys throws away the image of thieves lurking in ruins which comes at the very end of Book 3—an image that could serve as an emblem for the whole *Relation* and is very closely related to the emblematic transformation elaborated with deliberate rhetorical care in the dedication—demonstrates again, as in the Malta episode, his reluctance to direct his apparatus of symbolic interpretation at his own experiences. There is little in Sandys that corresponds to what we might call the impressionism of later travelers—that is, a set of techniques which develop the writer's impressions into personal poetic experience and/or a key to the spirit of the place.

It should be said at once that the sharpness of Sandys's eye is one of the real pleasures of this book. He is very observant of his surroundings, has a sense for significant detail, and can render visual effects with simplicity and acuity. He can also create elaborate and sustained effects, as his description of Constantinople shows (p. 31).

But Sandys's impressions are subordinated to descriptive intent: they are almost never indulged for their own sake, and the absence of picturesque or romantic values prevents their being accumulated in great quantities and organized into autonomous patterns of meaning. The details he records refer to facts or categories of more general interest, and this more or less direct reference justifies their inclusion. As in the confused passage from the end of Book 3, there is a level of generalization hovering above descriptive passages, or an ulterior descriptive intention running through them, pulling them away from the realm of direct personal experience, of sensory or emotional or aesthetic involvement. These ulterior motives are exactly what the literature of advice for travelers sought to inculcate. The modern reader may have the depressing feeling that this insures that Renaissance travelers will always be bound by the stereotypes they brought with them, that at most they will bring a little freshness and personal immediacy to the repetition of commonplaces and the collection of information under predictable heads. This is true of a great number of Renaissance travel writers, but it does not do justice to the vigor of Sandys's descriptions or the suavity with which he handles his materials. Here is Messina:

> The Citie is garnished with beautifull buildings, both publicke and priuate. *Venus, Neptune, Castor* and *Pollux* had here their Temples, whose ruines are now the foundations of Christian Churches. Diuers ancient statues are here yet to be seene. Throughout the Citie there are fountaines of fresh water: and towards the North end, the ruines of an old Aquaduct. In that end which turnes to the East, about the bottome of the bay, where the Citie is slender, and free from concourse of people, stands the Vice-roys Pallace, of no meane building, surrounded with delightfull gardens and orchards, to which the Arsenall adioyneth. . . . Here liue they in all abundance and delicacy, hauing more then enough of food, and fruites of all kinds; excellent wines, and snow in the summer to qualifie the heate therof, at a contemptible rate. The better sort are *Spanish* in attire, and the meanest artificers wife is clothed in silke: whereof an infinite quantity is made by the worme, and a part thereof wrought into stuffes (but rudely) by the workman. Eight thousand bailes of raw silke are yearely made in the Iland; and fiue thousand thereof fetcht from them (for, as hath bene said before, they will not trouble themselues to transport it) at the publicke Mart here kept, which lasteth all August, by the gallies of *Naples, Ostia, Ligorne,* and *Genoa:* during which time they are quitted from customes. The Gentlemen put their monies into the common table, (for which the Citie stands bound) and receiue it againe vpon their bills, according to their vses. For they dare not venture to keepe it in their houses, so ordinarily broken open by theeues (as are the shops and warehouses) for all their crosse-bard windowes, iron doores, locks, bolts, and barres on the inside: wherein, and in their priuate reuenges, no night doth

passe without murder. Euery euening they solace themselues along the Marine (a place left throughout betweene the Citie wall and the hauen) the men on horsebacke, and the women in large Carosses, being drawne with the slowest procession. There is to be seene the pride and beauties of the Citie. There haue they their play-houses, where the parts of women are acted by women, and too naturally passionated; which they forbeare not to frequent vpon Sundayes. [Pp. 245–46]

This passage is full of facts, virtually all of which are of the sort demanded by the writers of manuals for travelers, but they are so skillfully handled that even the economic data seems less like information for merchants than another side of the public life of the city, of its character. The beauty and color and passion and violence and indolence of Messina all emerge from this description and blend to create a whole which is not at all stereotyped or mechanical. The character of Messina as Sandys gives it seems to arise simply out of what he sees, and what he sees are the most salient, most visible and typical aspects of the town. He has not seen a mystical vision, or anything like it, and he seems to be describing a real place, not a transcendental entity.

But Sandys must have thought of cities as having something like a metaphysical soul. Barely four pages before he had quoted a poem by J. C. Scaliger in which a personified Syracusa meditates on her historical fate (p. 241)—this kind of prosopopeia is a persistent motif in humanist poetry. Just what is being personified cannot perhaps be defined with much conceptual precision, but the personification is a highly significant element in humanist thought about history. It suggests a mystical essence and destiny, a soul apart from the material body. The soul of a city (or country) is something which unfolds itself in history, builds itself monuments, is perhaps most clearly expressed through religious and mythological associations; it leaves its records in writing, in books. It is not something to be encountered in any street, or to be discovered by talking to the natives. (Which is why the reader meets so few people in Sandys's pages, though Sandys met so many on his trip.) This soul apparently constituted the primary significance of a place for Sandys; therefore he turns immediately to his learned materials when faced with a new place to be described. Sometimes the existing city can be shown to be a continued expression of this essence; more often there is a tragic recognition of difference.

In any case—and this is the point to be made here—one cannot arrive at this higher significance by contemplating one's own experiences and impressions. This language of public spiritual, historical and mythological symbols seems to be the only one in which reflection of the highest order can occur, and Sandys never employs it in his own person, without mediation—he expresses his meanings through a critical handling of the tradition he had mastered.

One could look for an explanation of this in Sandys's personality and talents, arguing that he simply lacked the poetic power, the belief in a transcendent principle within himself which would allow him to answer the inherited tradition and the complexities of the world with myths of his own. One could also argue that original mythmaking becomes progressively harder as a tradition grows older, and that Sandys comes at the very end of a very old one. Poems such as the one by Scaliger referred to above prove that it is not just a function of his being a modern rather than an ancient; but Sandys is late even with respect to Scaliger, and his Englishness is even more important than the intervening years in insulating him from the emotions which gave rise to such poems. Historical loss is his major theme, and we should not underestimate the seriousness with which he took it, but it does not touch him as it did the earlier, southern humanists; he has accepted it, the gestures he performs towards it are more restrained, he does not desperately try to force visions out of the ruins. Sandys is closer to the literature which embodies these attitudes than to any other (the most concentrated and developed expressions of the theme of historical loss outside of the dedication are in his translations of poems by Scaliger and Sannazaro), but he is just distant enough that he can work from it, incorporating it without needing to repeat it. The heightened rhetorical style used to express this facet of humanism is present as one of the many forms of knowledge and expression Sandys collects: it has become part of the content of his own style, which is set in a lower key and is designed to be flexible and comprehensive.

Whatever the truth or relevance of these suggestions, Sandys clearly chose a rhetorical stance which set him apart from the poets, the mythmakers. Although he wanted to be associated with them he did not want to be confused with them. The negative connotations of "fabling" were too present to his mind; his own authority was based in the credibility of his prose. His project was fundamentally one of mythmaking, but his myths are rationalized, and naturally expressed in prose. The poets have a major role to play in this project, which is really an elaboration of theirs, but in order to maintain the proper and profitable relation between poetry and prose the identity of the prose term must be kept intact, as factual and reliable. If Sandys were to indulge in conceits and fantasies of his own it would only confuse matters.

For the same reason Sandys shows remarkable restraint in assimilating his own experiences or present conditions to the inherited myths associated with a place. The passage about Baiae discussed above is an example of such restraint; he implies his point rather than enforces it. In other places he lets slip by obvious opportunities to achieve spectacular connections. Mythological material is usually introduced early on in Sandys's descriptions, along with etymologies and capsule histories, and often it is not invoked again. But the fact that it is separated from the rest of the account does not necessarily mean that it is disconnected; and the fact that it is not developed does not necessarily mean that it is dead learning. A writer of a later period, when mythological thinking was dead, would have to do something with such a reference in order to infuse some life into it. For Sandys the mythological significances are still very much present—they are not merely the product of his rhetoric. He could rely on his readers to bring a rich body of associations to such references, and he may also be relying on them to make for themselves the connections among the materials he assembles. The assemblages are so careful and the connections so obvious, that it is impossible to believe that Sandys was not planning them.

It is typical of Sandys to suggest relationships without defining them too precisely. He thought relationships of that kind were both indefinite and infinite; in the preface to the *Ovid* he explains that:

> In the Muthologie I haue rather followed (as fuller of delight and more vsefull) the varietie of mens seuerall conceptions, where they are not ouer-strained, then curiously examined their exact proprietie; which is to be borne-with in Fables and Allegories so as the principall parts of application resemble the grounde-worke.

His silences are often pregnant: he omits the process of interpretation entirely because once begun it could only be brought to an end arbitrarily, creating an illusion of completeness.

A good deal of what has been said about the mythological element is also true of a great number of the poetic passages Sandys quotes, even purely descriptive passages which have no mythological content. It has already been suggested that the authority of these passages makes them an inevitable part of Sandys's subject matter; they are also intimately connected with his procedures as extensions of his voice and sensibility, and are on the whole better integrated with his prose than the myths are. As instruments for description the Latin and Neo-Latin poetry Sandys uses exceeds anything possible in his prose in its formality, its pomp, its heightened imagery and diction, as well as its closer connections with the mythological tradition. The genuinely poetic effect of the *Relation* as a whole would be impossible without frequent recourse to this higher rhetorical mode. Given the conventions of the *Relation* it would seem unnatural for him to insert poetry of his own (he does so only once, the hymn composed at Christ's Sepulcher mentioned in "Deo Opt. Max."). What we get repeatedly is a rising motion in his prose which then gives way to someone else's poetry. This is the eruption of the New Mountain north of Naples:

> In the yeare of our Lord 1538, and on the nine-and-twentieth of September, when for certaine daies fore-going the countrey hereabout was so vexed with perpetuall earthquakes, as no one house was left so entire, as not to expect an immediat ruine: after that the sea had retired two hundred paces from the shore (leauing abundance of fish, and springs of fresh water rising in the bottome) this Mountaine visibly ascended about the second houre of the night with an hideous roring, horribly vomiting stones, and such store of cinders, as ouer-whelmed all the buildings hereabout, and the salubrious baths of *Tripergula* for so many ages celebrated, consumed the vines to ashes, killing birds and beasts: the fearefull inhabitants of *Putzol,* flying through the darke with their wiues and children; naked, defiled, crying out, and detest-

ing their calamities. Manifold mischiefes haue they suffered by the barbarous, yet none like this which Nature inflicted. But heare we it described by
Borgius:

> What gloomy fumes dayes glorious eye obscure!
> The pitchy lake effused through sulphury caues,
> Higher than AEtnas fires throwes flaming waues.
> Hath Phlegeton broke into Auerne, with grones
> Whirling the horrid flouds, and rumbling stones!
> The Baian waues resound . . . [P. 278]

The quotation is followed by a scientific explanation of the eruption, very
much in the style of the commentary on the first book of the *Metamorphoses.*
Sandys's prose is flexible enough to perform a number of tasks around this
eruption, vividly preparing for it and objectively analyzing it: it is only the
sublime moment of the eruption itself from which it backs away. (There is a
similar passage on p. 243 in which Virgil and Lucretius describe the eruption of
Aetna.)
Or here is a quieter example from Sandys's initial description of Sicily:

Vines, sugar-canes, hony, saffron, and fruites of all kinds it produceth:
mulberry trees to nourish their silke-wormes, whereof they make a great
income: quarries of porphyre, and serpentine. Hot bathes, riuers, and lakes
replenished with fish: amongst which there is one called *Lago de Goridan;*
formerly the nauell of *Sicilia,* for that in the midst of the Iland; but more
anciently *Pergus:* famous for the fabulous rape of *Proserpina,*

> Caysters slowly gliding waters beare
> Farre fewer singing swannes, then are heard here.
> Woods crowne the lake, and clothe the bankes about
> With leauy veiles, which Phoebus fiers keepe out:
> The boughs coole shade, the moist earth yeelds rare flowers:
> Here heate, nor cold, the death-lesse Spring deuours.

Ouid. M. 1.5

In this Iland is the farre-seene mountaine of AEtna: the shady *Eryx* sacred to
Venus, that gaue vnto her the name of *Erycine: Hybla,* clothed with thyme,
and so praised for hony. [P. 235]

The lines from Ovid are anything but a random association. They work in the
first place as a literal description of what Sicily looks like (still looks like) in
places. It also quietly introduces the familiar *topos* of the *locus amoenus,* one of
the archetypal forms in which landscapes can be perceived, and suggests that
that way of looking at Sicily is relevant to Sandys; especially relevant, of
course, because this is the very place where the archetype is anchored through
mythological and literary associations. It is easy to understand the significance
of the overwhelming wealth described in Sandys's first two sentences in the

light of this literary ideal—it becomes something much more dignified and important than a list of trade items. And we can accept the elevation of the final sentence quoted here because Sandys has demonstrated repeatedly on this page that we are moving over an epic landscape, to which epic style is merely appropriate.

Ovid is good for intimate landscapes such as this one, and of course myths and customs; Virgil for all the epic effects in their largest and most prestigious form (though Homer is the true source and should be referred to when possible); Horace for public moralizing; Lucan had written geographical descriptions of many places Sandys went in a high style which obviously appealed to him. Sandys had an eye for social detail and a biting wit which must not be unrelated to his reading of Martial; he found it difficult not to write satires, and one can sometimes feel him becoming Juvenalian half a page in advance of his citation of "the Satyr." These authors could serve as surrogate sensibilities because Sandys's sensibility—at least his literary one—had been developed under their influence. Sandys's awareness moves in counterpoint to theirs, sometimes in direct imitation, sometimes in opposition. As he travelled across their native ground it was inevitable that he would turn to their words to express sentiments common to both of them; and he may use them to express shared sentiments even where this immediate justification is missing.

But his relationship with the classical poets is not simply one of imitation and slavish deferral. He subjects them to criticism; at times (especially in Book 4) he has very harsh things to say about their civilization ("ignorant Antiquitie" etc.), and the poets can get drawn into the general condemnation. (For instance, Martial, whom he is using to construct a description of a Roman amphitheater and what went on in it—which horrifies him—, is called "that grosse flatterer" [p. 270].)

So Sandys uses the poets for a variety of purposes: as a source of information; as a repository of higher meanings not available to him through his personal experiences; as a means for achieving heightened effects impossible in the cooler medium of prose; as models for, and reinforcements of, his own attitudes; as the impetus and support for his own literary effects. Although their power exceeds his in various ways, nevertheless he is not overwhelmed by them, and manages not only to handle them critically but also to establish his own positions through opposition to them.

Some more general remarks can now be made about Sandys's use of literary materials and their relation to his role in the book. It should be clear that the classical references are neither merely ornamental nor the debris of a humanistic education, but are an absolutely central element in the understanding developed by the *Relation*. They are the nerves of its learnedness, not just external signs of it; they make the *Relation* the public and authoritative book it is. The representation of the eastern Mediterranean it contains is a collective one, in the production of which vast ranges of the cultural history of the West are brought into play. The plurality of Sandys's points of reference gives the world he describes a degree of clarity and solidity and spaciousness which was very unusual in its day and is in great contrast to the necessarily small and flickering circle of light his unlearned contemporaries could cast about them as they moved through a world in which everything was new to them, all relations uncertain.

The clarity of Sandys's representation is produced not so much by fixing a concrete object in a steady light, as by a smooth and careful and accurate movement from one view to another, an integration of perspectives creating depth of field. (So Purchas called him "a Learned Argus, seeing with the Eyes of many Authors".) And the solidity is the result, rather paradoxically, of watching the object in question—a city, an island, a custom—as it undergoes constant metamorphoses in the flux of history. The *Relation* is permeated throughout by the resonances of a profound cultural memory, with its traumas and continuities.

In a landscape so spacious and densely detailed the figure of the traveler is necessarily small and fleeting. To impose his own image on such materials would have seemed preposterous to Sandys, to organize all the themes contained in them around his brief passage equally hopeless, and to pretend to be re-creating the landscape out of his own imagination impertinent. Consequently the creative role of his subjectivity and hence the interest taken in Sandys the traveler is limited, and his presence intermittent.

But if the traveler keeps a low profile the author infuses his personal style and presence into everything; there is no dominant figure, no visible hero, but a strong sense of the mind (very personal, but whose personality is not an important issue) which is organizing the diverse materials of the book. The *Relation* has many sources and the world speaks to Sandys with many voices, but they are all translated into his very distinctive English. That the language is all Sandys's insures the continuity between his own prose and the poetry he is appropriating.

Sandys is always present as the center—in part to be defined in personal terms, in part in historical ones—towards which events, places, objects, and texts are drawn. As they approach this center they are translated, interpreted, criticized, coordinated with each other, commented upon, arranged in patterns. Within this process there is a constant mediation being performed between important sets of opposed terms: past and present, Latin and English, poetry and prose, public and personal. It is through this translation and mediation that the *Relation* generates its most important meanings. In the course of re-creating the past and the foreign a modern English identity is established, defined through hundreds of characteristic acts of assimilation, adjustment or rejection. The self-portrait gradually emerges from the arrangement of foreign materials and the stances taken toward them. The traveler and the author are both involved: if the traveler is often the more vivid, still he more often seems to be an extension of the author than the other way around. He is very consciously playing the role of field representative for the learned classes in England (as, in a comic mode, Tom Coryat went east with credentials drawn up in the Mermaid Tavern certifying him as the "Traveller for the English wits"); he always has their interests in mind, and his principal function is one of verification or modification of what is already known. His presence on the spot gives him special authority as the mouthpiece of the "threatening instructions" history presents to the English reader, but it would have been possible to draw the moral (though less interestingly) without leaving England.[8] Sandys's most important attitudes are taken up on a deeper basis than the reactions of a mere traveler—they are informed by the whole of his culture's stance towards the East and antiquity, a stance directly related to its most fundamental notions about itself and inextricably bound up with a canon of inherited literature. Sandys's unique value to his contemporaries was that his knowledge of this literature was as sharp and familiar as his knowledge of the East; he could maintain the same critical stance towards both and could slip effortlessly and almost without a change in tone from one realm to the other.

PART II

Four Forms of Historical Knowledge

3

Turkey

Superstition, without a vaile, is a deformed thing; For, as it addeth deformity to an Ape, to be so like a Man; So the Similitude of Superstition to Religion, makes it the more deformed.

Bacon, "Of Superstition," *Essays*

We cannot see or understand anything except through the medium of culturally determined structures; when we try to understand another culture the models we think with are inevitably those of our own. This has the double effect of inevitably distorting the culture under observation and, unless the observer brings a great deal of intellectual rigor or generosity to the task, of making that culture appear to be unnatural or defective, a distortion of the observer's own.

It was the humanists who inaugurated the attempt to capture another culture in its integrity, by trying to eliminate anachronisms from their understanding of the ancients. They were both rigorous and generous: they developed disciplines that revealed their distance and differences from the ancients, but only in order to establish a meaningful dialogue with them. Even when they disagreed with the ancients—and Sandys sometimes does so in very strong language—they maintaned an interest in what they were like, based in a strong sense of affinity and of inheritance. The problems arising from the religious question could be softened if not entirely resolved by finding in the differences between the Christian order and the pagan the measure of a divinely ordained historical evolution.

There was no such genetic relation with the Turks—the relation was one of stark opposition, not evolution. Studying Islam essentially meant defining the enemy. Islam was considered to be a Christian heresy, the difference between them here being measured not as an historical evolution but as a falling away from the divine truth. The religious element, which plays such a variety of roles in Sandys's thinking, is of overwhelming force in his consideration of Islam. Christianity is not just the nearest available model of religious behavior; it is an absolute standard of judgment, and judgment quickly takes on the meanings of salvation or damnation. The authority of Christianity as a model is so great, and its opposition to Islam so militant and absolute, that Islam is understood simply as its negative.

This sort of religious prejudice is an extreme (though not rare) form the interpretation of cultures can take; Sandys himself will provide us with other kinds of interpretation that are more disinterested and perhaps more self-conscious as intellectual procedures. Religious prejudice and religious hatred make this morally the least attractive part of the *Relation,* but if we want to know what Sandys thought we cannot blink at them. The way a comprehensive view of Turkish culture is produced through a combination of religious preju-dice and the budding sciences of culture is both interesting and instructive. Although Sandys probably would have maintained that an evaluation of Turk-ish culture ought to be based in a theological understanding, the largely secular terms in which his analysis is carried out tend to obscure that basis, so that we need to uncover the form of his understanding through interpretation.

Perhaps it should be emphasized that the object of this study is not to establish George Sandys's personal guilt. His prejudice and hatred were thor-oughly orthodox and institutionalized in the whole corpus of European knowl-edge of Islam. It would have been very difficult for him to have thought otherwise. Sandys could be harsh when he thought it was necessary, and his hatred is real enough, but it is usually an expression of Christian fervor rather than of personal malice. As a responsible intellectual he carried out his con-demnation of Islam with all the sophistication and energy he could muster, but read in the context of anti-Islamic polemic he comes across as calm, sane, and almost sweet-tempered.

Book 1 takes Sandys from Venice to Istanbul, with some brief stops on Greek islands. The center of the book is taken up with an extended formal description of the Turks, arranged under the headings of "The Turkish his-tory," "policy," "forces," "Mahomet," "The Mahometan religion," "the Turk-ish clergy," "the Turkish manners etc.," and finally a sketch of Sultan Achmet (pp. 42–76). The discussions of Muhammad and Islam form the intellectual center of Sandys's consideration of the Turks, and are therefore the appropriate place to begin.

Sandys's biography of Muhammad is as uncharitable as most written in the Renaissance.

> Their Morall and Ecclesiasticall lawes, the *Turkes* do receiue from *Mahomet* the *Saracen* lawgiuer: a man of obscure parentage. . . . he became a Captaine of certain voluntary Arabians that followed the Emperour Hera-clius in his *Persian* warres. Who falling into a mutinie . . . a part of them chose *Mahomet* for their ring-leader, who had aggrauated their discontents, and confirmed them in their rebellion. But being disdained by the better sort for the basenesse of his birth; to auoide ensuing contempt, he gaue it out, that he attained not to that honour by military fauour, but by diuine appoint-

ment. That he was sent by God to giue a new law vnto mankind; and by force of armes to reduce the world vnto his obedience. That he was the last of the Prophets; being greater than Christ, as Christ was greater then *Moses.* Two years together he liued in a caue, not farre distant from *Mecha;* where he compiled his damnable doctrine, by the helpe of one *Sergius* a *Nestorian* Monke, and *Abdalla* a Iew (containing a hodgepodge of sundry religions;) which he first communicated to his wife, perswading her that it was de-liuered him by the Angell *Gabriel* . . . His new religion by little and little he diuulged in *Mecha;* countenanced by the powerful alliance which he had by his sundry wiues; and followed by many of the vulgar, allured with the libertie thereof, and delighted with the noveltie . . . Meane of stature he was, & euill proportioned: hauing euer a scald head, which (as some say) made him weare a white shash continually; now worne by his sectaries. Being much subject to the falling sicknesse, he made them beleeue that it was a propheticall trance; and that then he conuersed with the Angell *Gabriel.* Hauing also taught a Pigeon to feed at his eare, affirming it to be the holy Ghost, which informed him in diuine precepts. Not vnlike to *Numa's* feigned familiaritie with *AEgeria;* and *Pythagoras* his Eagle: whose policie perhaps he imitated: whereby as they the *Romans* and *Crotonians;* so drew he the grosse *Arabians* to a superstitious obedience. For he had a subtill wit, though viciously employed; being naturally inclined to all villanies: amongst the rest, so insatiably lecherous, that he countenanced his incontinency with a law: wherein he declared it, not onely to be no crime to couple with whom soeuer he liked, but an act of high honor to the partie, and insuring sanctitie. Thus planted he his irreligious religion, being much assisted by the iniquities of those times: the Christian estate then miserably diuided by multitudes of heresies. So that the disunitie of the professors made many to suspect the profession, and to embrace a doctrine so indulgent to their affections. [Pp. 52–53]

Sandys's themes—Muhammad as wily imposter and natural rebel, his threat to the social and political order, his religion as a compilation of Christian and Jewish elements, and his laws as an excuse for sexual license in himself and his followers—as well as the facts, distortions, and outright inventions through which they were developed, were all inherited from the Middle Ages.[1] Some of the major themes can be traced as far back as St. John of Damascus in the early 8th century; they hold sway through the 17th century (the best biography at the end of the century was Humphrey Prideaux's, entitled *The Nature of Imposture fully displayed in the life of Mahomet* [1697]) and into the Enlighten-ment. Sandys is if anything less offensive than most of his contemporaries.[2]

As Muhammad lacked integrity as man and prophet, so the Quran lacked integrity as a text—this too was an old objection, but it was felt with new force in the Renaissance.[3]

The Alcoran, which containeth the summe of their religion, is written in *Arabicke* rhime, without due proportion of numbers: and must neither be

written nor read by them in any other language. Besides, the positiue doctrine (to it selfe contradictory) farced with fables, visions, Legends, and
relations. Nor it is at this day the same that was written by *Mahomet*,
(although so credited to be by the vulgar) many things being secretly put in,
and thrust out, and some of the repugnancies reconciled by the succeeding
Caliphs. And *Mahomet* the second is said to haue altered it much, and added
much to it. [Pp. 53–54]

The whole religion and everything connected with it is presented as a distortion of something else, implicitly or explicitly. The brief account of Islamic
doctrine that follows is taken up with noting points of similarity and difference
with Christian theology. Especially of interest are issues that had been disputed
within the Christian church, or myths which seem especially ridiculous when
compared with the truth of Christian revelation. These comparisons are made
silently: Sandys's summary is presented as an outline of Islamic doctrine,
though it is little more than a catalogue of selected points on which Islam is
heretical with respect to Christianity. Major facets of Islam, such as the special
status of the Quran, are ignored; there is little attempt to grasp it as a system of
thought. "Now their opinions of the end of the world, of Paradise, and of hell;
exceede the vanity of dreames, and all old wiues fables" (p. 58), Sandys writes,
although those opinions seem no more extravagant than (and actually not much
different from) those of the book of *Revelations*. Because he will not understand them as anything more, Islamic beliefs appear to be at best the products
of an unrestrained and undirected imagination; at worst, they seem to have
been deliberately designed to appeal to that most untrustworthy faculty of our
minds.

Sandys's argument culminates in an attack on the Muslim Paradise:

It is to be more then coniectured, that *Mahomet* grounded his deuised Paradise, vpon the Poets inuention of *Elisium*. For thus *Tibullus* describeth the
one.

> For that my heart to loue still easly yeelds,
> Loue shall conduct me to th'Elisian fields.
> There songs and dances reuell: choice birds fly
> From tree to tree, warbling sweete melody.
> The wild shrubs bring forth Casia: euery where
> The bounteous soyle doth fragrant Roses beare.
> Youths intermixt with maids disport at ease
> Incountring still in loues sweet skirmiges.
>
> Eleg. 1.1, Eleg. 3.

And *Mahomet* promiseth to the possessors of the other, magnificent pallaces
spread all ouer with silke carpets; flowry fields, and christalline riuers; trees
of gold still flourishing, pleasing the eye with their goodly formes, and the
taste with their fruites,

Which being pluckt, to others place resigne,
And still the rich twigs with like mettall shine.

Virg. AEn. 1.6

Vnder whose fragrant shades they shall spend the course of their happy time with amarous virgins, who shall alone regard their particular louers: not such as haue liued in this world, but created of purpose; with great blacke eyes, and beautifull as the Hyacinth. They daily shall haue their lost virginities restored: euer young, (continuing there, as here at fifteene, and the men as at thirty) and euer free from naturall pollutions. Boyes of diuine feature shall minister vnto them, and set before them all variety of delicate viands. [Pp. 58–59]

What shocks Sandys so deeply about this Paradise is not simply that it is plagiarized, but that it is even more extravagantly sensual than the fantasies of the ancients. Derivation from a classical source is often a sign of respectability, but here the very nature of the soul and its relation to the body is in question, and the cleavage between Christian and pagan is as absolute as it can be.

The poets were merely unenlightened, but Muhammad, "who by sensuall doctrine sought to draw the rude world to follow him" (p. 59), is crafty and calculating, aiming at extending his wordly power at the cost of seducing his followers into spiritual perdition. His paradise is a demonic parody of the real thing, not simply a distortion of it; like Spenser's evil magicians he manipulates the symbols he finds at his disposal into a system that allures but destroys. To read such a system correctly is to recognize the evil principal that underlies it.[4]

Sandys anticipates the objection that a more positive reading is possible; to meet it he introduces the figure of "*Auicen* that great Philosopher and Physitian, who flourished about foure hundred and fifty yeares since, when *Mahometisme* had not yet vtterly extinguished all good literature" (p. 59). The idea of using a reasonable Muslim against Islam is by no means original with Sandys—much of what Europe knew about Islam it had learned from converts, thereby fixing the type in its imagination, and there was a recurring faith among Europeans that all that was required to convert Muslims was to reason with them (although their conceptions of the grounds on which such reasoning could be based were, with few exceptions, extremely naive). Avicenna's prestige and his connection with ancient and modern learning in the West all made him ripe for conversion. In Sandys's hands this ploy is no less superficial than it usually was, and cannot be taken as the sign of a serious interest in Islamic thought. In fact the life, books, and ideas attributed to "Auicen" are those of Averroës;[5] and it is symptomatic of the quality of European knowledge of Islamic philosophy that this error went uncorrected through all the subsequent editions of the *Relation*.

Sandys demonstrates that Islam constricted "Auicen"'s mind like an ill-fitting garment, using him to deny its intellectual and spiritual credibility:

For although as a *Mahometan*, in his bookes *De Anima* and *De Almahad*, addressed particularly to a *Mahometan* Prince, he extolleth *Mahomet* highly, as being the *seale* of diuine *lawes* and the *last of the Prophets;* excusing his sensuall felicities in the life to come, as meerely allegoricall, and necessarily fitted to rude and vulgar capacities . . . yet besides that this excuse is so fauourable & large, that it may extend as well vnto all Idolaters, and in briefe to the iustifying of the absurdest errours, it is in a point of doctrine so contrary to his owne opinion as nothing can be more. For *Auicen* himselfe in the aforesaid bookes, doth esteeme so vilely of the body, that he pronounceth bodily pleasures to be false and base; and that the soules being in the body is contrarie to true beatitude. . . . So strangely may wise men be besotted with faction, to excuse and commend the teaching of absurd errours euen by themselues condemned, and to lay an aspersion vpon the purity of diuine doctrine, in that vnfit to be so communicated to the ignorant, as if Truth were to maske her selfe to please beastiall Ignorance, and Ignorance not rather to be enlightned by degrees, and drawne vp to behold the Truth. But now this *Auicen*, laying downe for a while his outward person of a *Mahometan*, and putting on the habite of a Philosopher; in his Metaphysicks seemeth to make a flat opposition betweene the truth of their faith receiued from their Prophet, and the truth of vnderstanding by demonstrative argument. And saith, in effect, that their law and prophesie deliuered by *Mahomet*, which taught that God himselfe at the resurrection should haue a body, placeth the happinesse of the life to come in bodily delights. But wise Theologians, saith he, haue with greater desire pursued spirituall pleasures proper to the soule: and for this corporal felicity, although it should be bestowed vpon them, would not esteeme it in comparison of the other, whereby the mind is conioyned to the first truth, which is God. And here he neuer mentioneth that strained excuse of an allegory: but with just indignation and some acerbity of speech, detesteth that grosse opinion broched in their law, which placeth the predominance of euerlasting felicity in the basenes of sensuality, and in that lowe voluptuousnes; and saith that a prudent & vnderstanding man, may not thinke that all delight is like the delight of an Asse. . . . This being his better aduised & more sincere discourse, it vtterly excludeth his former excuse of an allegory: whose right vse being, by plaine and sensible allusions to draw vp the vnderstanding to an apprehension of diuine things, represented in those similitudes: the course held by *Mahomet* worketh a clene contrary effect; and drowneth their vnderstanding part and affection in the hope and loue of these corporall pleasures. Whereby it is true that he greatly enlarged his owne earthly dominion: but by this judgment euen of *Auicen* withheld his followers from the true felicity. And it is worthy obseruation, that in the iudgment of *Auicen* one thing is true in their faith, & the contrary in pure & demonstratiue reason. Wheras (to the honor of Christian Religion be it spoken) it is confessed by all, & enacted by a Councel, that it is an errour to say, one thing is true in Theology, & in Philosophy the contrary. For the truths of religion are many times aboue reason, but neuer against it. [Pp. 59–60]

"Avicen" puts on "his outward person of a *Mahometan*" only when addressing a prince: for him, as for Muhammad, the positive value of Islam is as a tool to be manipulated for worldly ends. As a philosopher it is entirely unacceptable to him. Sandys has created here an argument for the impossibility of understanding Islam. It is not the truth and because it is repugnant to reason it cannot be interpreted as a version of the truth. Nothing can be known through Islam, and nothing can or should be known about it as an intellectual system except that it is a perversion, a falling away from the intelligible. Allegory is the normal method of rescuing symbol systems that cannot be taken literally, but Islam is bad allegory, leading the mind in exactly the wrong direction. This refusal to understand is all the more extraordinary when compared with Sandys's extension of allegorical interpretations to "all Idolaters": his patient explication of ancient religious beliefs, his interpretations of the signs of ancient Egyptian wisdom, his allegorizations of the Book of Nature and, most obviously, his interpretations of the myths in the classical poets—all of which are less promising materials and much further removed from the forms of his own culture. It is of course the very proximity of the Christian truth that prevents him from seeing Islam as anything but an aberration. In the other cases he can see a sign of the truth or a movement towards it, confused or misdirected as it may be; but Islam is understood as a departure from the truth, both historically and intellectually, and this movement away from the known is thought to be a movement away from the mind itself, and from the transcendent principles the mind may know. Islam cannot be understood as a religion, only as a fraud.

Just as there was a long tradition of explicating classical materials and the Book of Nature, there was a tradition of rejecting Islam as a matter of principle. The principle is clearly articulated in the ringing condemnation with which Sandys ends his consideration of "the Mahometan Religion":

> So that we may now conclude, that the *Mahometan* religion, being deriued from a person in life so wicked, so wordly in his proiects, in his prosecutions of them so disloyall, trecherous, & cruel; being grounded vpon fables and false reuelations, repugnant to sound reason, & that wisedome which the Diuine hand hath imprinted in his workes; alluring men with those inchantments of fleshly pleasures, permitted in this life and promised for the life ensuing; being also supported with tyranny and the sword (for it is death to speake there against it;) and lastly, where it is planted rooting out all vertue, all wisedome and science, and in summe all liberty and ciuility; and laying the earth so waste, dispeopled and vninhabited, that neither it came from God (saue as a scourge by permission) neither can bring them to God that follow it. [P. 60]

One of the first ideas Christendom had about Muhammad was that he might be the Devil; that idea is still just beneath the surface in Sandys. He is the Prince of this world, a scourge by permission, obscenely parodying and perverting good religions to evil ends, leading men to spiritual perdition through the senses. A whole string of the most basic oppositions in the Western mind are tracked onto that of Christianity and Islam: spiritual felicity and corporeal pleasures, truth and earthly dominion, reason and superstition.

It is hard to imagine a more sweeping rejection of the values of an alien civilization, or a more thorough recapitulation of all the impediments to cross-cultural understanding generated by centuries of fear and hostility. How completely did this religious hatred dominate European perception of Turkish civilization as a whole?

That civilization was strong enough to compel Europeans' attention and even admiration for selected aspects of it, in spite of the vehement religious opposition to the whole. It was widely admitted that Turkish society was more efficiently organized, more harmonious in its working, more cleanly in appearance, possibly more pious in its religious observance and more charitable.[6] (We can feel in these admissions what a squalid and violent place Renaissance Europe was.) So Sandys notes

> they liue with themselues in such exemplary concord, that during the time that I remained amongst them (it being aboue three quarters of a yeare) I neuer saw *Mahometan* offer violence to a *Mahometan;* nor breake into ill language: but if they so chance to do, a third will reproue him, with Fie *Mussel-men,* fall out! and all is appeased. [p. 58]

That a devilish religion should give rise to admirable results was felt to be paradoxical.[7] It was also acutely embarrassing to Christians, whose possession of truth exceeded their virtue. For centuries the virtue of Muslims was used in homiletic and polemical contexts to shame Christians: Sir John Mandeville, for instance, inserts a long tirade against the wickedness and hypocrisy of Christendom into the mouth of the Soldan of Babylon.[8] Throughout the Renaissance Islam was used as a weapon of controversy by both Catholics and Protestants.[9] But like the virtue of the Noble Savage, the virtue of the Muslim could form a familiar if anomalous element in the moral thought of the West without leading to a crisis of faith or conscience in any but a few rare cases. It is hard to detect any traces of fundamental doubt in George Sandys.

Such a limited recognition of value in Turkish culture might not shake the ultimate and overwhelming hostility to what was perceived as its value system, but it at least allowed Europeans to enlarge their vision of the Turks, to take an interest in an increasing number of aspects of their life. This was coupled with the doubtless more powerful strategic necessity of collecting information about the enemy. (The standard justification for learning about Islam was that it would facilitate the conversion of Muslims.) Gradually a large body of information was accumulated, which for its organization required the most advanced and complex intellectual patterns Europe had—more or less those it used for itself.

This is most true of knowledge of Turkish governmental and military institutions. Sandys's description of "The Turkish Policy" may be loaded with invective, and may present it as the antithesis of European systems in much the same way Islam is made the antithesis of Christianity, but his knowledge is detailed and accurate in a way his account of religion is not.[10]

But the barbarous policie whereby this tyrannie is sustained, doth differ from all other: guided by the heads, and strengthened by the hands of his slaues, who thinke it as great an honour to be so, as they do with vs that serue in the Courts of Princes: the naturall *Turke* (to be so called a reproach) being rarely employed in command or seruice: amongst whom there is no nobility of blood, no knowne parentage, kindred, nor hereditary possessions: but are as it were of the *Sultans* creation, depending vpon him onely for their sustenance and preferments. Who disposeth, as well as their liues as their fortunes, by no other rule then of his will . . . [P. 47]

For his description Sandys could refer to a number of sophisticated analyses of the Turkish system, the products of the new political science. Machiavelli, for instance, had approached it simply as a type of government from which certain military and political consequences could be reliably inferred (*The Prince*, Chapter 4). But Sandys never aims at this kind of detachment: for him the Turkish policy is "damnably politicke," a system held together only by terror and violence, and therefore the opposite of the reciprocal bond between ruler and ruled outlined at the beginning of his Dedication to Prince Charles. Like Islamic allegory, Turkish policy is a violation of the proper Neo-Platonic relation between higher and lower, and hence its only possible fruit is moral degradation in ruler and ruled alike.

Such a supposition does not encourage analysis of the institutions through which the tyranny is enforced. That such an analysis is included probably reflects Sandys's awareness of the work of the aggressively secular students of comparative government, and his desire for intellectual respectability; it is not especially a reflection of his personal purposes. We can notice in his account a retreat from the aims of political analysis into moral and even metaphysical judgment on the one hand, and a more concrete, visual representation on the other. He turns the Turkish government into a pageant, giving detailed descriptions of the dress and accouterments of the various sorts of soldiers and officers, finally describing all the parts of the Turkish army in its marching order (pp. 50–51). He will return again to another depiction of a procession, the Sultan's passage from his Seraglio to Aya Sofia, saying "there is not in the world to be seene a greater spectacle of humane glory, and (if so I may speake) of sublimated manhood" (p. 75). He is creating an image of the Turks, a theatrical representation,[11] and in doing so he is free to admire their magnificent theatricalism. Sandys is most generous with his attention when he is describing the physical manifestations of Turkish culture—styles of dress, workmanship, the beauty of the women. The resulting portraits are rich and appealing, and must be taken as contributing a good deal to a realistic notion of who the Turks are. But if the Turks are brought onto the stage of the reader's imagination in splendid array, they do not do or say much once they are there: the sense of their identity is acutely limited. The generosity of attention to their appearance is possible because their appearance has for the moment been disassociated from all values except aesthetic (visual, theatrical) ones.[12] The object of the description is inert, and therefore not threatening.

An analogous shift from analysis in depth to more vivid if shallower values can be discerned in Sandys's history of the Turks. It is a swift chronicle of conquest, dissension, military prowess, and meteoric rise and fall, delivered in a heightened style:

> To *Calizasthlan* he gaue the regall Citie of *Iconium*, with the vnder Prouinces: to *Iagupasan, Amasia* and *Ancyra,* with part of *Cappadocia,* and the territories adiacent: but to *Dadune* he gaue the ample cities of *Cesarea* and *Sebastia,* and all the spacious countries adioining: the whole being lateley a parcell of the declining *Greek* Empire. But these ambitious brethren, like the sonnes of Earth, drew their swords on each other. The eldest dispossessing *Dadune* of his patrimony . . . [P. 43]

The level of factual detail is unnecessarily high for a survey of this kind—the motive is not the desire for information but relish for the narrative and stylistic values of the story. Europeans had a style for which Eastern despots were the perfect content (cf., obviously, *Tamburlaine*), their names providing barbaric splendor and their deeds the occasion for bombast and easy moralizing. History is reduced to plot; there is no sense of time, of historical periods. The characters likewise are colorful and extravagant but have no depth. The history resembles an abstract of a romance.

I shall have a great deal to say about the forms of Sandys's historical awareness later on. We shall find that there is a generic thinness in these historical sketches, no matter whose history is being recounted. This history of the Turks is striking because of its unusually happy union of form and exotic context. But the significant thing about Sandys's treatment of Turkish history is that there is almost nothing to supplement this rather barren chronicle except the story of Muhammad's heresy. Compared with this understanding of the histories of other places and peoples it is clearly substandard. When faced with the task of writing the history of the Turks or another alien culture, Sandys abandons or radically restricts two of the central features of humanist historiography. One is the perception of cultural particularity, and of the changes that take place in a culture from one epoch to another; the other is the emphasis on the element of moral choice and human creativity in history.[13] The force of these ideas in Sandys is admittedly somewhat tempered, since his interest in history is predominantly as a source of *exempla* ("threatening instructions"), and this tends to override attention to the organic development of cultures and the historical particularity of different epochs.[14] For him the will enters on a primarily personal and individual level.

And Sandys had an interest (again, one that was common in the Renaissance as well as in antiquity) in occult patternings of history—prophecies, oracles, symmetries—which tends to qualify the sense of history as the product of the human will (and sometimes makes the meaning of the threatening instructions a little uncertain). In general (there are exceptions) occult patterns are repressed in the vicinity of his own civilization and that of classical antiquity, where his specifically historical thinking is strongest, and blossom around the periphery of his historical awareness. Occult patterns were especially appropriate in the theological context in which Islam was seen. The history of the Turkish capital is loaded with occult elements:

This Citie by destinie appointed, and by nature seated for Soueraigntie, was first the seate of the *Romane* Emperours, then of the *Greeke,* as now it is of the *Turkish.* Built by *Constantine* the sonne of *Helena,* and lost by *Constantine* the sonne of another Helena (a *Gregorie* then Bishop, whose first Bishop was a *Gregorie)* to *Mahomet* the second, in the yeare 1453. with the slaughter of her people, and destruction of her magnificent structures. The like may be obserued of the Romane Emperors; whose first was *Augustus,* and whose last was *Augustulus.* So haue they a prophesie that *Mahomet* shall lose it. [Pp. 29–30]

In spite of these moralizing and occult elements in his thinking, which tend to reduce all histories to the same form, there is a distinct difference in the way history and ideas about culture enter into Sandys's treatment of European and non-European peoples, a contrast that can be noted between the section on the Turks and the one on the Greeks that follows it. Sandys's thinking about the Greeks is dominated by his knowledge of their past and what it meant:

A Nation once so excellent, that their precepts and examples do still remaine as approoued Canons to direct the mind that endevoureth vertue. Admirable in arts, and glorious in armes; famous for government, affectors of freedome, euery way noble: and to whom the rest of the world were reputed *Barbarians.* But now their knowledge is conuerted, as I may say, into affected ignorance, (for they haue no schooles of learning amongst them) their liberty into contented slauery, hauing lost their minds with their Empire. For so base they are, as thought it is that they had rather remaine as they be, then endure a temporary trouble by preuailing succours; but would with the *Israelites* repine at their deliuerers. [P. 77]

The Greeks have removed themselves from the historical stage, and have forgotten their past—"For not a *Greeke* can satisfie the Inquirer in the history of their owne calamities. So supine negligent are they, or perhaps so wise, as of passed euils to endeauour a forgetfulnesse" (p. 36). But Sandys is in a position to make detailed comparisons between their past and present states, and does so in a number of areas: national character, dress, drinking customs, language, funeral rites. If anything, the ancient customs dominate his attention. Continuities and changes are noted, admixture of foreign elements is differentiated from their own "supine retchlessnesse" as a cause of change. Although they are taken to task for abandoning the values and civilization that once were theirs (and are now in large part Sandys's), continuity is not always a good thing: immoderate drinking is still a vice, pagan superstitions are an unwanted pollution of Christian rites, and Lucian's satire remains as relevant to modern Greek funerals as to ancient ones. What the Greeks are now is understood as an historical evolution from their past, to be explained as the product both of circumstances and of their own will. They have certainly declined from their original greatness, but they are still thoroughly comprehensible and likable, still accorded (if with condescension) an honored place in the European family.

The Turks on the other hand are too firmly locked into their identity as the antithesis of Europe and the scourge of God to promote either the use of history as a tool for interpreting Turkish culture, or a search for the central values that give that culture coherence. There is no attempt to develop the few stray remarks about changes in Turkish customs into a cultural history that would supplement the rather empty military/political history discussed above. In fact these remarks are, with perhaps one or two exceptions,[15] concerned with a decline, a sign of degeneracy, often also an infraction of their own law: they have begun to drink, to take bribes, to take native Turks into the Janissaries, and so on. It is significant that the most extensive discussion of this decline occurs in the middle of the section on "The Turkish Forces":

> And surely it is to be hoped that their greatness is not onely at the height, but neare an extreme precipitation: the body being growne too monstrous for the head; the *Sultans* vnwarlicke, and neuere accompanying their armies in person; the souldier corrupted with ease and liberty, drowned in prohibited wine, enfeebled with the continuall conuerse of women, and generally lapsed from their former austerity of life, and simplicity of manners. Their valours now meeting on all sides with opposition; hauing of late giuen no increase to their dominions: & Empire so got, when it ceasseth to increase, doth begin to diminish. Lastly, in that it hath exceeded the obserued period of Tyrannie, for such is their Empire. [P. 50]

The signs of decay were real and significant, but Sandys's application of historical laws to this evidence owes more to wishful thinking than to the reconstruction of the course of Turkish history. Nor is there any attempt to place the Turks in the context of Islamic civilization as a whole, to explore, for instance, the statement that "Auicen" flourished "when *Mahometisme* had not yet vtterly extinguished all good literature." The internal history of Islam is of no interest; the inevitable tendency of "Mahometisme" is obviously (from what Sandys has said) to destroy civilization, it being only a matter of time.

The failure to locate a vital center in Turkish culture is clear in the rather careless and informal survey with which Sandys closes his consideration of the "Nation in generall."

> To speak a word or two of their sciences and trades: some of them haue some little knowledge in Philosophie. Necessitie hath taught them Physicke; rather had from experience than the grounds of Art. In Astronomie they haue some insight: and many there are that undertake to tell fortunes. . . .
> They haue a good gift in Poetry, wherein they chant their amours in the

Persian tongue to vile musicke; yet are they forbidden so to do by their law: Gitternes, Harpes and Recorders being their principall instruments. But their lowd instruments do rather affright then delight the hearing. On a time the *Grand Signior* was persuaded to heare some choise *Italian* musicke: but the foolish Musitians (whose wit lay onely in the ends of their fingers) spent so much time in vnseasonable tuning, that he commanded them to avoid; belike esteeming the rest to be answerable. [P. 72]

The irony of this little anecdote does not go deep enough to lead Sandys to doubt his judgment of the vileness of Turkish music. Throughout this paragraph Sandys runs through a catalogue of the arts and sciences as constituted in Europe, looking for Turkish equivalents. Sometimes the Turks have little or nothing with which to respond to this cultural questionnaire; their own arts tend to be overlooked. It is impossible, for instance, to get a sense of the beauty and importance of Turkish caligraphy and the decorative arts from Sandys's scattered comments. The Turks are allowed to express their rejection of the study of Rhetoric and Logic, though in terms that were long familiar, not to say stale, in the West: "They study not Rhetorick, as sufficiently therein instructed by nature; nor Logick, since it serues as well to delude as informe; and that wisedome (according to the opinion of the Epicures) may be comprehended in plaine and direct expressions." Sandys's tendency to assimilate foreign ideas to an element in his own intellectual heritage has already been mentioned.[16] Here the force of the objections is neutralized by their apparent familiarity, and the sense that they are recurrent objections obviates the need to understand them in the context of a particular culture; though in fact Sandys probably does understand them in the context of a fundamental rejection of all learning, again based in their faulty religion: "Printing they reiect; perhaps for feare lest the vniuersality of learning should subuert their false grounded religion and policy; which is better preserued by an ignorant obedience."

Sandys concludes this survey with a description of the Turk's moral character: lazy but excessively covetous, with the will but fortunately not the wit to deceive, liable to violate contracts with Christians if it suits them, but dealing with each other in ready money only, which keeps them out of court. In line with what precedes it, this is the Turkish character as seen from a European standpoint—specifically, that of a Christian merchant trying to do business with them.

In many of Sandys's contemporaries this characterization would pass for complete—compare, for instance, William Lithgow.[17] Sandys knew it was not: for him the Turk is a more complex character, capable of playing many roles besides that of deceitful trading partner, some of them having little or no relation to European interests. His perception of the social harmony prevailing among the Turks has been mentioned. It has also been suggested that if the Turk was a figure of many (or at least several) sides, he was also hollow within. That hollowness is the result of a failure to give him a voice, to let him express himself, and to come to terms with what he might have to say (admittedly a terribly difficult task, given the language and cultural barriers); but it is also the expression of what was seen as an essential emptiness at the heart of the Turkish character. Sandys saw in the Turk a psychological abyss that corresponds to the metaphysical abyss in the Muslim's religion, the moral abyss in his politics, the failure to establish a rational and creative center in his culture. The natural tendency of the Turkish mind is to stupefy itself. They listen to readings of the Quran "as if they were intranced"; when praying

> some shak[e] their heads incessantly, vntill they turne giddie: perhaps an imitation of the supposed trances (but natural infirmitie) of their Prophet. And they haue an Order of Monkes, who are called *Dervishes*, whom I haue often seene to dance in their Mosques on Tuesdayes and Fridayes, many together, to the sound of barbarous musicke; dances that consist of con-tinuall turnings, vntill at a certaine stroke they fall vpon the earth; and lying along like beasts, are thought to be rapt in spirit vnto celestiall conuersations. [P. 55]

For sport they swing on ropes,

> perhaps affected in that it stupifies the senses for a season: the cause that *opium* is so much in request, and of their foresaid shaking of their heads, and continued turnings. In regard whereof, they haue such as haue lost their wits, and naturall idiots, in high veneration, as men rauished in spirit, and taken from themselues, as it were to the fellowship of Angels. These they honour with the title of Saints, lodge them in their Temples, some of them going almost starke naked . . . [P. 56]

> The *Turkes* are also incredible takers of Opium, whereof the lesser *Asia* affordeth them plenty: carrying it about them both in peace and in warre; which they say expelleth all feare, and makes them couragious: but I rather thinke giddy headed, and turbulent dreamers; by them, as should seeme by what hath bene said, religiously affected. And perhaps for the selfe same cause they also delight in Tabacco . . . [P. 66]

This tendency is clearly linked to their propensity for losing themselves in the unrestrained imaginative and sensual license of Islam.

This is very different from Sandys's portrayal of the Greeks, mindless and foolish as they have become. We can recognize them as a sanguine type, with their unthinking merriment, their love of dancing and drinking. Travelers were encouraged (e.g. in the manuals published for their instruction) to produce stereotypes of the characters of various nations, using a vocabulary closely allied to that of the four humors: Spaniards are grave, melancholic, and jealous, Italians are quick-witted, deceitful, and love display, Germans are heavy, and given to drink and music.[18] Such stereotypes are obviously linked to those found on the stage and in other popular literature. As in the theory of the four humors, some combinations of characteristics are more attractive than others; some indicate a diseased temperament. But all are comfortably within the realm of human nature: they are simply variations on a theme, on a norm which is flexible and is taken so much for granted that it need not be stated.

This language of character is applied to non-European peoples as well, but they are too different to be contained within it. Perhaps it should be said that the problem is not thought of in terms of race[19]—even the Turkish tendency to stupefy the senses, the most physiologically related of the cultural attributes Sandys discusses, is not described as a racial characteristic, as it might be later. If the Turks seem less than fully human it is because the word has begun to describe an ideal—an ideal to be realized through work, through culture—rather than a zoological classification. And if it were simply a matter of culture, the assumption of a rough equivalence of cultures might encourage the deciphering and interpretation of even the most bizarre behavior. But there was a decisive religious element as well—there could be no equivalence between Christian and Muslim cultures.

A culture that is radically foreign can only be understood by trying to grasp it in its own terms, at least as a preliminary strategy, and it is this that Sandys does not do. A theological condemnation stops the questioning, stops the search for the right questions. So the pervasive perception of Turkish culture as a distortion of the true or the normal or the European leads Sandys to elaborate a coherent description of that culture, with each aspect based on a similar negation or failure or emptiness, all of them springing ultimately from the devilish imposture of Muhammad. The medieval notion of Muhammad and Islam as the antithesis of Christ and Christianity has intersected a more sophisticated attention to cultural phenomena and analysis of their interrelationships to produce this portrait of a civilization that is complex, powerful, in some ways advanced, yet nearly devoid of positive values and irrevocably cut off from God. Its meaning can therefore not be understood as a European culture can be understood.

This then is one way in which Sandys reads foreign cultures. Its application is not limited to the Turks or even to Muslims, though it is not worked out on such a grand scale (or theorized about at such length) for any other people. We can see most of its features recur in the descriptions of the Jews (pp. 146–49), or the Christian sects celebrating Easter in the Temple of Christ's Sepulcher in Jerusalem (pp. 171–73), or the Copts (pp. 110–11). History is not used to explain much of anything about them (as it was with the Greeks), although a great deal of historical knowledge may be in play. As it is applied to non-European peoples, history tends to be reduced to a registration of their foreignness, a story about how they became so different. Often—as with Islam—this difference can be derived from a single heresiarch, who in his apostasy creates a pattern which his culture will continue to exemplify in perpetuity; the moral life of his followers is frozen into a static repetition of his exemplary action.

Such thinking is mythic in character; it is of a piece with the orthodox

Biblical explanation of the origins and diversity and diffusion of cultures through the catastrophic moral choices of Adam, Cain, Noah's children, and the builders of the Tower of Babel. It is very different from the project of humanist historiography and philology, which had begun to describe history as the evolution through time of a complex but integrated cultural whole, and as a field for creative action. (Though the humanist project certainly had a mythic structure of its own.) So we find that the rather stiff figures populating the borders of the European imagination, with their heraldic accouterments and their limited, obsessively repetitious gestures, are animated by a different—and feebler—spirit than that which moves the main figures on the central stage.

To expect anything else would be naïve. Giving a foreigner a life and voice that are anything more than those of a puppet requires an enormous amount of labor. The motivation for doing so is mysterious and far from natural—some would say it is unique to a certain moment in the history of the West.

> The Renaissance initiated an entirely new phase in the development of Islamic and Middle Eastern studies in the Western world. Perhaps the most important new factor was a kind of intellectual curiosity that is still unique in human history. For until that time, no comparable desire had been felt and no effort made, to study and understand alien, still less hostile, civilizations. Many societies have tried to study their predecessors, those to which they feel they owe something, those from which they perceive themselves to be derived. Societies under the domination of an alien and stronger culture have usually been impelled, by force or otherwise, to learn the languages and try to understand the ways of those who dominate them. Societies, in a word, have studied their masters, in both senses of the word. . . . But the kind of effort to study remote and alien cultures made by Europe (and later by the overseas daughters of Europe) from Renaisance times onwards, represents something new and totally different.[20]

This is undoubtedly a great event, but we must be careful not to make this kind of statement too quickly. In any case the notion of pure intellectual curiosity should be examined with a severity commensurate with its importance. Expressions of pure intellectual curiosity about alien cultures are hard to find in the Renaissance, and approaching it with this noble ideal in mind is more apt to lead to disappointment and recriminations than to better understanding. The kind of analysis of the structure and motivations of discourse about the foreign that Edward Said proposes in the Introduction to his *Orientalism* seems at least equally useful and necessary (though the unacknowledged ideal of pure knowledge haunts his book and accounts for some of its accusatory tone). Sandys's conservativeness, his concern with scholarly prestige, his reliance on written (and therefore European) sources rather than on direct contact with the natives, and his restricted imaginative sympathy all make him especially liable to the kind of "Orientalism" Said describes. For all the intellectual curiosity and careful observation and good workmanship of his account of Islam and the

Turks, it is still based on a paradigm (to use Thomas S. Kuhn's phrase) that shuts off in advance a great deal, and qualifies the notion of pure curiosity. A threshold would have to be crossed before a new paradigm could be adopted, a threshold which Blount saw and wanted to cross. But Sandys did not, and in this he is altogether representative of the mainstream of European thought about the East.

4

Egypt

O Egypt, Egypt, of thy religion nothing will remain but an empty tale, which thine own children in time to come will not believe; nothing will be left but graven words, and only the stones will tell of thy piety. And so the Gods will depart from mankind.

> *Hermes Trismegistus,*
> *Asclepius* III, 24b, in the
> *Hermetica,* translated by Walter Scott

All the characteristic attitudes and prejudices outlined in the last chapter operate in Egypt as well. If anything Sandys has less respect for the oppressed than for the Turkish oppressors—"A people breathes not more sauage and nastie" (p. 110) is his opinion of the Egyptian *fellaheen.* His responses are proportionately more hostile as the more hostile and disordered environment of an Egypt occupied but not really governed by the Turks bore on him personally. Outside Cairo Egypt was very dangerous—the Janissaries rode with the fuses of their matchlocks lit. Book 2 of the *Relation* is full of little icons of injustice: "At the gate they tooke a Madein a head, for our selues and our asses, so indifferently do they prize vs" (p. 115). On the caravan trip to the Holy Land a dangerous episode is quietly turned into allegory:

> The *Subassee* of *Sahia* inuited himselfe to our tent; who feeding on such prouision as we had, would in conclusion haue fed vpon vs; had not our Commandement (which stood vs in foure *Shariffes*) from the Bassa of Cairo, and the fauour of the Captain by means of our Physition, protected vs: otherwise, right or wrong had bin but a silly plea to barbarous couetousnesse armed with power. [P. 138]

The history of Egypt culminates with a character study of the current Pasha ("sowre and inflexible"), intermingled with descriptions of the slaughter that accompanied his ascension, and the tortures with which he perpetuated his rule.

Not everything about modern Egypt offended him, of course. He admired

the architecture of Cairo: "But the priuate buildings are not worth the men-
tioning, if compared to the publicke: of which the Mosques exceede in
magnificency: the stones of many being curiously carued without, supported
with pillars of marble; adorned with what Art can deuise, and their Religion
tollerate." (p. 119) "What Art can deuise": the mosques of Cairo compel
unlimited admiration, but that admiration is never expressed more fully than
this, and so they never become really present to the reader. Cairo comes
through less clearly than any of the other major cities of the *Relation*, perhaps
because it corresponds least well to the humanists' ideas about cities: it was a
nearly impenetrable labyrinth, without the sort of public space or civic structure a European would expect. But Cairo was one of the few places where the
aristocracies of East and West met socially, and of this we hear nothing, though
Sandys spent three weeks there. (See Blount's *Voyage,* pp. 40–2. He gives a
dazzling description of the interior of a Cairo palace, and of his reception
there.) The Cairo Sandys gives us is public and external: magnificent if decaying buildings, festivals, street singers, trained animals, all the bazaar exotica.
Some scenes are borrowed from Leo Africanus.

His attention was elsewhere. Like most tourists since Herodotus he came to
see the Nile, palm trees, crocodiles, hieroglyphs, the Pyramids, the Sphinx.
The natural world, the Egypt of the Greeks and Romans, and the pharaonic
monuments compete with the contemporary scene for his attention, and perhaps they win out. Sandys's Egypt is a mosaic of these elements. The mosaic
pattern prevents the sort of singleness of purpose that informed the First Book
on Turkey—nowhere is a thesis less apparent. Each detail seems to bring its
own meaning and its own gratifications, each an emblem luminous with its
own light. Yet this pattern has a logic of its own, and implications for the ideas
of history in play in the *Relation.* The argument of this chapter is that Sandys's
tendency to create emblems (usually moral ones) comes into its own in this
Book, and becomes the basic unit of meaning. This is possible because Egyptian history as a whole is not otherwise organized by any very powerful pattern; and this sort of emblematizing tends in turn to disintegrate more
historical modes of understanding. It also tends to envelop the natural as well
as the human worlds. A subtheme will be the historical coloring and anachronisms introduced by Sandys's classicism—this too, strangely enough, also
spills into the natural world.

Let us begin where Sandys begins, with geography. In the classical tradition
about Egypt a fascination with the place itself is at least as important as any
opinions about its culture, and so it is for Sandys. On his arrival from Turkey
he suspends his narration (very much in the manner of Herodotus) to give us a
geographical survey, a long discussion of the traditional problems associated
with the Nile, and descriptions of the exotic flora and fauna; only then does he
turn to Egyptian history and ethnography, and finally, twenty-two pages after
he began, resumes his trip.

This turn towards the geographical had been extravagantly staged by Lucan.

In Book 10 of the *Pharsalia* Caesar is feasted in decadent splendor by Cleopatra; when he is sated he asks an Egyptian priest to tell him about the antiquities and culture of Egypt, but it is really the Nile that fires his imagination.

> Sed, cum tanta meo vivat sub pectore virtus,
> Tantus amor veri, nihil est, quod noscere malim
> Quantum fluvii causas per saecula tanta latentes
> Ignotumque caput: spes sit mihi certa videndi
> Niliacos fontes, bellum civile relinquam.[1]

Caesar does not get a straight answer—if he thought one was possible he doubtless would not have made his extraordinary offer—but the priest gives him an account of the descent of the river that Sandys uses extensively.

It is significant that he does so. Sandys's Nile is a work of art; his ability to transform geography into an imaginative experience is one of the real pleasures of the *Relation*. Like the illustration we are given of the statue of "Nilus" brought to Rome by Vespasian (p. 95), Sandys's Nile is built on classical models (besides Lucan, Pliny is probably a stylistic influence), and has the qualities we associate with Baroque art: splendor, weight, an effect of volume and motion. At every turn it implies the fame and grandeur of the river.

> . . . it passeth, wandering through spacious deserts, and multitudes of king-domes; not seldome seeming to affect his forsaken fountaines: now dispersed into ample lakes, and againe recollecting his extrauagant waters, which often deuide to make fortunate Ilands, (amongst which *Meroes* the fairest and most famous) appearing euer more great than violent.

> But when rough crags, and head-long cataracts
> Receiue his fals: mad that each rocke distracts
> His former vnimpeached sourse; he laues
> The stars with spume, all tremble with his waues,
> The mountaine roares; and foaming with high spite
> Immantleth his vnuanquisht waues in white.
>
> Lucan, 1.10. [P. 93]

The ancient vexed problem of the cause of the Nile's flooding is as much a literary occasion as the course of the river. "But amongst the hidden mysteries of Nature, there is none more wonderful than the ouerflowing of this Riuer" (p. 94). It too is given a monumental classical dress. Assisting at this mystery are the AEgyptians with their hieroglyphs (by which Sandys probably means Horapollo 1, 21), Anaxagoras, AEsculus, Euripides, Lucan, Horace, Thales, Lucretius, Herodotus, Diodorus Siculus, Callimachus, various anonymous figures, and several moderns (pp. 97–99). (And probably Seneca too, though he is not named.) Sandys thinks Diodorus is right in attributing the flooding to rains in Ethiopia, but he is curiously unemphatic in asserting this solution: the mystery is more a *topos* to be rehearsed than a problem to be solved, so opinions that were discredited by Herodotus continue to be collected and discredited.[2]

He has another style for plants and animals, not quite so high, whose affinities are with earlier Renaissance art. Nature is emblematized and moralized, shaped into patterns of correspondence and sufficiency. On the stylistic level the classical antecedents are less clear, but Sandys frankly and rather engagingly states his preference for traditional lore. He tells how the Ichneumon jumps into the crocodile's mouth and bores through his entrails:

> This though now little spoken of, in times past was deliuered for a truth, euen by the *AEgyptians* themselues: who gaue diuine honour vnto the *Icnumon* for the benefite he did them in the destroying of that serpent. And true no doubt but it is, though perhaps not much obserued by the barbarous. [Pp. 100–1]

(This may well be a jab at Pierre Belon, who declines to repeat all the old ichneumon lore at just this point [*Observations*, 2, p. 96r].)

Nature is a complex of measured symbolic values and mysterious connections. The whole ecology of Egypt is quasi-magical in this way: the crocodile in particular is at the center of a web of symmetries and antipathies.

> The female laies an hundred egges; as many dayes they are hatching; and as many yeares they liue that do liue the longest, continually growing. Where she layeth, there is (as they write) the vtermost limits of the succeeding ouerflow: Nature hauing endued them with that wonderfull prescience, to auoide the inconueniences, and yet to enjoy the benefit of the riuer. By the figure therefore of a Crocodile, Prouidence was by the *AEgyptians*, hieroglyphically expressed. Between the Dolphins & these there is a deadly antipathy. *Babillus*, a man highly commended by *Seneca*, obtaining the gouernement of *AEgypt*, reported that he saw at the mouth of *Nilus* then called *Heraclioticum*, a scole of Dolphins rushing vp the riuer, and encountred by a sort of Crocodiles, fighting as it were for soueraignty; vanquished at length by those milde, and harmelesse creatures, who swimming vnder did cut their bellies with their spiny fins: and destroying many, made the rest to flie, as ouerthrowne in battell. A creature fearfull of the bold, and bold vpon the fearfull. [P. 100]

The Book of Nature is especially legible in Egypt, largely because the hieroglyphs retain their privileged function of providing a transition from Nature to script. The hieroglyphs and other forms of emblems are not historical curiosities but real methods of apprehending nature. Sandys seems very much at home in this Neo-Platonic world, but again his use of his materials is characteristic. In *Isis and Osiris* 75 the crocodiles lay sixty eggs, hatch in sixty days, and live sixty years; and Plutarch points out that "the number sixty is the first of measures for such persons as concern themselves with the heavenly bodies." Sandys also declines to repeat that the crocodile is held to be a representation of God since he has no tongue ("for the Divine Word has no need of a voice"), and that he has a membrane covering his eyes which allows him to see without being seen, a prerogative that belongs to God. Sandys hesitates to let the crocodile lead to ultimate cosmic terms, or to an occult connection with knowledge. The full flower of Neo-Platonism has been pruned—the reflections and analogies tend to be contained within a more narrowly conceived realm of nature.

The great exception to this is that everything tends to turn into moral allegory. This turn is paralleled by the movement from the Egyptian hieroglyph to more general kinds of symbolism—here provided by Seneca's friend, who expands what might have been originally expressed as a hieroglyph into a fuller rhetorical form, the allegorical battle. The same movement from the metaphysical to the moral and from the Egyptian to the classical occurs with the Palm, which the Egyptians thought "to be the perfect image of a man; and by the same represented him. . . . And because the Palme is neuer to be suppressed, but shooteth vp against all opposition, the boughs thereof haue bin proposed as rewards for such as were either victorious in armes or exercises. . . .", a custom instituted by Theseus and illustrated out of Horace (p. 102). Sandys's Egypt is largely built up of classical commentary crystalized around an original Egyptian sign; this gives a curiously classical cast even to Egypt's natural history, and its effects elsewhere are even more pronounced. The anachronism generated by his classicism is pervasive, and is more apparent than the decontextualizing effect of his emblem-mongering. It is the anachronism most appropriate to a humanist. It is an intellectual habit, but also an aesthetic predilection, and we perhaps feel it most strongly when it intervenes between us and the style or feeling we expect to get from ancient Egypt. It can be paralleled by his engraver's visual illustrations, which make no attempt to capture the aesthetic effect of Egyptian art or to stress its foreign and archaic qualities. There were practical reasons for this: Renaissance artists had practically no opportunities to see genuine Egyptian art. But it is also true that they ignored the examples that were available, like the statuettes Sandys brought back and gave to John Tradescant, which are illustrated on his page 133 in a style that is not at all Egyptian. Similarly the sample hieroglyph on his page 105 is not one Sandys saw, but the one everyone read about in Plutarch's *Isis and Osiris* 32; the artist simply drew pictures of an infant, a falcon, a fish, and so on in the style that came naturally to him. His hippopotamus is an illustration of the etymology of the word in Greek: a horse (with an aquatic tail) swimming in a river. This draws a reprimand from Sandys in the margin, but the intervention of a Greek word between the Renaissance observer and the Egyptian thing is paradigmatic.

The whole of the representation of ancient Egypt has the same classical cast. Again, there were severe constraints on the possibilities: virtually everything

the Renaissance knew or could know about ancient Egypt was derived from
classical sources, so the natural tendency was simply to re-create the inherited
representation, with its stylistic and intellectual coherence intact. As will be
seen below, Sandys follows the classical tradition in viewing Egypt from the
standpoint of its contributions to Greece. But in many other instances Sandys's
classicizing is more clearly a matter of choice than of necessity. He explains the
methods of embalming the mummies at Memphis:

> Their ceremonies (which were many) performed, they laid the corps in a
> boate, to be wafted ouer *Acherusia*, a lake on the South of the Citie, by one
> onely whom they called *Charon:* which gaue to *Orpheus* the inuention of his
> infernall Ferri-man: an ill fauoured slouenly fellow, as should seem by *Virgil:*
>
>> Charon grim Ferri-man, these streames doth guard,
>> Vglily nastie: his huge hoarie beard
>> Knit vp in elfe-locks: staring-fiery-eyde:
>> With robe on beastly shoulders hung, knot-tide.
>>
>> *AEn.* 1.6
>
> About his lake stood the shady Temple of *Hecate,* with the Ports of *Cocytus*
> and *Obliuion,* separated by barres of brasse: the originall of like fables.
> When landed on the other side, the body was brought before certaine
> Iudges; to whom if conuinced of an euil life, they depriued it of buriall; if
> otherwise, they suffered it to be interred as aforesaid. So sumptuous were
> they in these houses of death, so carefull to preserue their carcasses. For-
> somuch as the soule, knowing it selfe by diuine instinct immortall, doth
> desire that the body (her beloued companion) might enjoy (as far forth as
> may be) the like felicitie: giuing by erecting such loftie Pyramides, and those
> dues of funerall, all possible eternitie. Neither was the losse of this lesse
> feared, then the obtaining coueted: insomuch that the Kings of *Aegypt* accus-
> tomed to aw their subjects (to them a most powerfull curbe, and a strong
> prouokement) by threatening to depriue them of sepulture. The terrour of
> this made *Hector* to flie, the onely feare and care of the dying *Mezentius:*
> [quotes *Aeneid* 10, 901–6] [Pp. 134–35][3]

The anachronism in this passage has several effects. One is to draw Egyptian
funeral customs into the circle of the comprehensible, by assimilating them to a
classical model. What they do is a natural result of a true principle they have
discovered (the immmortality of the soul), and it is easy to be tolerant of these
ideas because they are in Virgil, were held by the heroes of our civilization. The
mythological syncretism displayed two pages earlier ("In this way the Temple
of *Apis* [which is the same with *Osiris*] as *Osiris* with *Nilus, Bacchus, Apollo,*
&c. For vnder seuerall names and figures they expressed the diuers faculties of
one Deitie . . .") has the same effect.
A second effect, perhaps the most interesting, is that the fables of the Greeks
are given a home, a referent that gives them a kernel of literal truth. This is a
Euhemeristic interpretation, and aims at constructing a cultural history. The

derivation of Greco-Roman culture from Egypt is reiterated in a way that increases Egyptian prestige as it explicates the beliefs of classical antiquity.

But if the classical fable is re-placed in Egypt, it tends to displace the original: the Virgilian illustrations effectively obscure the Egyptian customs (Cf. p. 104, where the Egyptians' supposed belief in the transmigration of souls is smothered by Pythagoras.) Bacon wrote of the fables recorded by the classical poets as being "light airs breathing out of better times, that were caught from the traditions of more ancient nations and so received into the flutes and trumpets of the Greeks."[4] He tried to hear the original melody, but could not. But Sandys's ear was attuned to the classical strain, to the virtual exclusion of any other.

The Greek and Roman experience of Egypt was long and complex, even if in some ways surprisingly shallow; there was in any event a considerable range of positions in classical thinking about Egypt, and this range was available to the Renaissance. One of the strains of opinion in classical thought bears considerable resemblance to the Christian hostility to the Turks. Egypt is the archetype of the foreign; it provokes religious, moral, and aesthetic revulsion; and this powerful opposition may be the occasion for self-definition on the part of the European. So in the center of Aeneas's shield is portrayed the battle of Actium, the supreme moment of the assertion of Roman Imperial identity, and above the fleets of Octavius and Antony is a theomachy between the splendid great gods of Rome and the misshapen deities of Egypt: "The monster-Gods, Anubis barking, buckle / With Neptune, Venus, Pallas" (*Aeneid,* 8, 698–99). And so Juvenal's Fifteenth Satire—"What honor brain-sick AEgypt to things vile / Affoordeth, who not knows?"—recounts an incident of cannibalism brought on by a religious quarrel, reflects on the general degeneracy of the Egyptians, and then tries to define Roman virtue in opposition to their appalling immorality.[5]

Equally there were those in the Renaissance who read Egyptian civilization as a false system manipulated by impostors—an idea Sandys also had about Islam. So Ralegh, for instance, held that Egyptian religion was a corruption of the truth, an abasement of the object of worship from God to men, animals, and the elements, a fabling of true ancient history into Idols of mythology, a perversion of the pure monotheism of "*AEgyptian* Hermes . . . all being at length by deuilish pollicie of the *AEgyptian* Priests purposely obscured; who inuented new Gods, and those innumerable, best sorting (as the Deuill perswaded them) with vulgar capacities, and fittest to keepe in awe and order their common people."[6]

Everyone agreed that the Egyptian kings and priests deserved to be famous for their ability to keep the common people in awe and order, though the quality of that fame depended on the writer's religious politics. The Catholic Louis le Roy spoke sympathetically of the priests' manipulations, and gave them credit for the idea of establishing revenues for the priesthood.[7] For the Deist Sir Henry Blount, the Egyptian religion was a "superstition," a "juggling," and its priests were impostors, but this was to be expected in any organized religion, and "Therefore it is not hypocrisie, but a necessary regard to the vaine nature of man, which forces most religions to muffle toward the vulgar."[8] He seems scrupulously to avoid saying anything about the Egyptian superstition that could not also be said about Catholicism. In other circles Egypt was the type of spiritual bondage, a land whose civilization was advanced, but which had to be escaped from physically and transcended spiritually.[9]

The majority opinion was moderate, and felt free to appreciate what was accepted neutrally as Egypt's contribution to the history of civilization. If there was disagreement about the need for priestly manipulation, there was little about the need for political organization and repression, which the Egyptians were also thought to have inaugurated. Typically these were seen as linked, two aspects of the fundamental repression that makes civilization possible. Sandys credits the legendary king Busiris with both: he

> select[ed] the people vnto seuerall callings, and caused them to intend those onely; whereby they became most excellent in their particular faculties. He possessed them first with the adoration of the Gods; emboldening and awing their minds with a being after death, happy or vnhappy, according to the good or bad committed in the present: and instituted the honouring of contemptible things . . . [P. 103]

Once Sandys begins giving the Egyptians credit for their cultural contributions he does not stop until he has given away nearly all of Western civilization, from the Quadrivium to the works of the Greek culture heroes:

> The *Aegyptians* first inuented Arithmeticke, Musicke, and Geometry; and by reason of the perpetuall serenitie of the aire, found out the course of the Sunne and the starres, their constellation, risings, aspects, and influences; diuiding by the same the year into moneths, and grounding their diuinations vpon their hidden properties. Moreouer from the *Aegyptians*, *Orpheus*, and *Homer*, haue fetcht their hymnes and fables of the Gods; *Pythagoras*, *Eudoxus*, and *Democritus*, their Philosophie: *Lycurgus*, *Solon*, and *Plato*, the forme of their gouernments: by which they all in their seuerall kinds haue eternized their memories. Their letters were inuented by *Mercury*, who writ from the right hand to the left; as do all the *Africans*. But in holy things especially they expressed their conceits by Hieroglyphicks; which consist of significant figures: whereof there yet are many to be seen, though hardly to be interpreted. [P. 104][10]

Of all the strands of Egypt's reputation this is the most important for Sandys, and it is the oldest—it is already fully developed in Herodotus. This honor roll of inventions was often repeated in antiquity, though there was surprisingly little investigation of the culture that had benefited the Greeks so much.[11] To a great extent the meaning of Egyptian civilization was established by focusing on the moment at which its wisdom crossed the Mediterranean to Greece. There was a strong sense of inheritance, but this did not help much to reconstruct ancient Egypt, which was in large part drained of its own specific meaning in the process of absorption, and in a too easy assumption of familiarity. Music is an Egyptian invention, but there is little effort to distinguish Egyptian music from Greek.

We might call this a failure of cultural history, though of course the kind of cultural history we look for scarcely existed in the Renaissance. Partly the problem is inherent in the Renaissance genres of history writing: the formal historical narrative is a rather thin chronicle of great names and political events, while a richer understanding of the ancient culture is embodied in antiquarian treatment of objects and customs.[12] Meanwhile a history of the evolving moral character of the Egyptians is isolated from the other historical materials: "The *AEgyptians* of the middle times, were a people degenerating from the worth of their ancestors; prone to innouations, deuoted to luxury; cowardly cruell; naturally addicted to scoffe, and to cauill, detracting from whatsoeuer was gracious and eminent" (pp. 108–9). Just how this element is to be integrated with the others is unclear, or what its force as historical explanation is meant to be.

The history of Egypt is of endless and inglorious degeneration, a process which does not lend itself to a comprehensive narrative. Indeed it is hard to find events of compelling interest in it (though there is Cleopatra). The very length of its history makes it difficult to create a shaping historical myth. Rome falls, Byzantium is taken, Israel is swept away in a holocaust, but the history of Egypt is not informed by any such tension. The tension in the other cases is at once dramatic and moral ("threatening instructions"); it may also be political (Greece groans under the yoke of the barbarian, the Holy Land under the yoke of the infidel). The myth provides an impetus and a form for understanding as well as a story: Islam is a perversion historically and ontologically; the myths of the loss of Greece and Rome and of the purity of the early Church demand myths of restoration, a whole project entailing historical disciplines and the attempt to recapture and relive an ethos.

There was an historical myth for Egypt that Sandys fails to adopt—that of hermeticism. Like humanism and the Reformation, it was an historical movement, trying to recover the purity of a golden age—in this case, the *prisca theologia*, the secret knowledge Hermes Trismegistus shared with Moses, the seers of ancient Persia and Babylon, and the Greek poets. But Frances Yates begins her *Giordano Bruno and the Hermetic Tradition* by noticing the massive irony of the hermeticists' bad scholarship. Their historical knowledge was uniformly wrong: Hermes Trismegistus never existed; they misdated their sacred texts; the scraps of debased Greek philosophy the *Corpus Hermeticum* contained were thought to be the origins of that philosophy. "This huge historical error was to have amazing results."

In Chapter Nine she draws a clear distinction between "the humanist tradition," which she also calls "pure" or "Latin" humanism, and a Greek, hermetical, magical tradition. Now, enforcing this distinction would create an unacceptable division in the ranks of the humanists; in fact the humanists and the hermeticists were often not different people. But her distinction works very well for my purposes. Pure humanism is the invention of Petrarch: it is based on the recovery of Latin texts, good chronology, good philology, and the desire to return to

> the golden age of Latin rhetoric as represented by Cicero, the proficiency in literary and historical studies which a Ciceronian speech represents, its exquisite Latin style, the dignified way of life in a well-organized society, which is its framework. . . . The humanist's bent is in the direction of literature and history; he sets an immense value on rhetoric and good literary style. The bent of the other tradition is towards philosophy, theology, and also science (at the stage of magic).[13]

This other tradition is inspired by the "recovery of the Greek texts and their ensuing new philosophical revelation in the Fifteenth Century." Its ideal was no longer a civilized life in a civic community, but man as Magus, with the divine creative power within him.

Although the Greek phase follows the Latin it does not replace it—Erasmus is an example of pure humanism.

> Both by its critical scholarship and by its historical and social approach to man and his problems, an atmosphere of unadulterated humanism is not one which is congenial to the Magus and his pretensions. But the atmosphere very rarely was unadulterated and elements from the one tradition infiltrated into the other.
> Perhaps the clearest case of such infiltration is that of the hieroglyphs.[14]

The hieroglyphs infiltrated even the arch-humanist Erasmus, and George Sandys as well, who is another excellent example of pure humanism. He was no hermeticist, but the lore about hieroglyphs had since antiquity been in the more or less unchallenged custody of the Neo-Platonists, and the hieroglyphs had become absorbed into an emblematizing tradition—and habit of mind—that was very much Sandys's own.[15] To understand this we need to rehearse very briefly the strange life of the hieroglyphs in European thought.

The misapprehension of Egyptian thought and the hieroglyphs in particular by the Greeks and then the Romans is astonishing in light of the level of professed interest in them and the ease with which accurate knowledge could have been obtained. (The Christian misapprehension of Islam pales in comparison.) None of the writers on hieroglyphs bothered to acquaint himself with the Egyptian language, without which the script is incomprehensible, or even with the distinction between the various elements of the script. They were often correctly informed about the meaning of specific hieroglyphs (though they were also often wrong, and sometimes mistook ornamental motifs and conventional religious symbols for hieroglyphs); but they never understood the true relation between the words and the pictures, nor could they explain how a collection of symbolic pictures could be combined to form sentences. Virtually all their examples of hieroglyphs were of single symbols.[16]

Plutarch's *Isis and Osiris* is a good (and important—Sandys uses it extensively, as everyone else had) example of what happened when Egyptian symbols fell into the hands of Greek philosophers. He begins with the large and generous assumption that everything in Egyptian religion is not only intelligible, but worthy of respect and admiration. He is then faced with the formidable task of rendering it into the forms acceptable to a Greek Platonist:

> Nothing that is irrational or fabulous or prompted by superstition, as some believe, has ever been given a place in their rites, but in them are some things that have moral and practical values, and others that are not without their share in the refinements of history or natural science, as, for example, that which has to do with the onion.[17]

The need for interpretation is desperate ("you must not think that any of these tales [about the gods] actually happened in the manner in which they are related," 11); and Plutarch is led into a meditation on the correct use of the main forms of interpretation that had been developed for the Greek myths: Euhemerism, physical interpretation, and syncretism. There is need for fastidious care, but if understood correctly Egypt provides a valuable system of religious symbols (67–68).

But immediately there is an irreconcilable conflict between the proper (Greek) understanding and what the Egyptians actually do: the result is that Plutarch backs off considerably from his original claim. Most (not all) Greeks say correctly that various animals are sacred to the gods, but most Egyptians "in doing service to the animals themselves and in treating them as gods, have not only fulfilled their sacred offices with ridicule and derision, but this is the least of the evils connected with their silly practices" (71).

So we see the limitations of this kind of thinking: even Plutarch's generous mind found the reality of Egypt unacceptable. The best way of handling Egypt was to maintain a respectful distance, expressing admiration for the power and antiquity of the civilization and gratitude for the legacy it left the Greeks, and sanitizing a set of religious symbols with Platonic philosophy. More intimate knowledge was not rewarding. The integration of the Egyptian symbols with cultural actuality, with history, was a task which it would be pointless and ungracious to explore.

Diodorus Siculus attached this metaphorical and symbolic conception to the hieroglyphs, and Plotinus (*Enneades* 5, 8, 6) provided the mystical theory which governed their interpretation until the 18th century. He stated what Plato had seemed to suggest, that while art panders to the physical seeing that corresponds to discursive thought, the apprehension of the hieroglyphs corresponds to the immediate intuition of Ideas. "Thus each picture was a kind of understanding and wisdom and substance, given all at once, and not discursive reasoning and deliberation."[18] The hieroglyphs were written in a kind of code to exclude the vulgar, but to the initiate they afforded an insight into the transcendental nature of things, an insight that was the result of divine inspiration and illumination rather than of reasoning or reflection. Moreover they were perfect illustrations of the Neo-Platonic conception that all things in the world were inherently symbolic.[19]

So the explanation for the Greek ignorance of the real nature of the hieroglyphs is that

> what interested the Greeks was not Egyptian writing at all; but from their own "Platonic" interpretation of the relation between sign and meaning in Egyptian hieroglyphs, grew the idea of the existence of a true symbolic system of writing in which abstract notions and ideas could be expressed by means of concrete pictures of material objects.[20]

This dream of a perfect language of signs bewitched the humanists of 15th century Florence[21]—ironically enough, since the great humanist discovery had been the historicity of language. Obviously a complete symbolic language required more symbols than those found in Horapollo, so more were invented by men like Francesco Colonna and Valeriano. Alciati's *Emblemata* (1531) helped spread the vogue for emblems, which by now had a pronounced moral and ethical cast which was foreign to the original Egyptian hieroglyphs.[22] They were now a vehicle for practical allegory, often not very serious allegory, and the further the craze for emblem books and "devices" spread, the more trivial they became. As the hieroglyphs became absorbed into the iconographical and ornamental vocabulary of Western art, the Egyptian originals were lost sight of; when illustrating them Renaissance artists simply took them over into their own style, with no attempt to reproduce the originals, which in any case were almost always unavailable. It was not until almost Sandys's time that the first attempts were made to distinguish the original Egyptian hieroglyphs from the Renaissance inventions.[23]

What has all this to do with George Sandys and his Egypt? He was clearly not a hermeticist: no hermeticist would write a sentence such as this: "Aboue all they honoured *Isis* and *Osiris*, which fable (too tedious for our professed brevity) contained sundry allegories" (p. 103). Or this on the flooding of the Nile:

> Wherefore no maruell though ignorant and superstitious antiquity, vnder the name of *Osyris* adored this Riuer, which affoorded them so many benefits; and such as not apprehended were thought supernaturall. Thus where couered with water, it is no vnpleasant sight to behold the townes appearing

like little Ilands; the people passing and repassing by boate, and not seldome swimming: who the lesse they see of their country, the more is their comfort. [P. 97]

This last is perhaps sufficient witness to Sandys's appetite for positive knowledge, which hermeticism could hardly gratify; it shows him rejecting the historical myth of a golden age of ancient wisdom; its tone is antithetical to the kind of religious enthusiasm inspired by the ancient symbols that gives "the *Hermetica* a unity which they entirely lack as a thought system."[24] This passage also demonstrates the extent to which he was willing to rely on his own eye and wit rather than on the mystic authority of the ancient wisdom. The balance between them is decisive in determining the character of the Egypt he evokes.

His formal discussion of the hieroglyphs is brief, and comes as part of the discussion of Egypt's cultural inventions.

But in holy things especially they expressed their conceits by Hieroglyphicks; which consist of significant figures: whereof there yet are many to be seen, though hardly to be interpreted. One I will produce for an example, said to be pourtrayed within the porch of *Minerua's* Temple in the Citie of *Sai:* [Here he inserts the anachronistic depiction based on Plutarch discussed above.] The Infant signified those that enter into the world; and the old man those that go out of it: the Falcon, God; the Fish, hatred; because they hated fish that bred in the Sea, which symbolized Typhon: and by the Riuer-horse, murder, impudence, violence, and iniustice; for they say that he killeth his sire, and rauisheth his owne dam: which put together importeth; *O you that enter the world, and go out of it; God hateth iniustice.* [Pp. 105–6]

That he relies on the literary tradition rather than collecting new hieroglyphs suggests the limits of his archaeological curiosity; "though hardly to be interpreted" disclaims at least any personal initiation into the Egyptian mysteries, and perhaps expresses scepticism about all readings of the hieroglyphs; the word "conceits" seems to deny any direct and privileged relation between the hieroglyphs and a symbolic universe. It is significant that he has chosen an example that links several symbols together to form a message, and that the message is moral—both of which features are, as we have seen, very rare.

The beginning of the Preface to the Ovid translation will further elucidate matters.

Since it should be the principall end in publishing of Bookes, to informe the understanding, direct the will, and temper the affections; in this second Edition of my Translation, I have attempted (with what successe I submit to the Reader) to collect out of sundrie Authors the Philosophicall sense of these fables of Ovid, if I may call them his, when most of them are more ancient than any extant Author, or perhaps then Letters themselves; before which, as they expressed their Conceptions in Hieroglyphickes, so did they their Philosophie and Divinitie under Fables and Parables: a way not un-trod

by the sacred Pen-men; as by the prudent Law-givers, in their reducing of
the old World to civilitie, leaving behind a deeper impression, then can be
made by the livelesse precepts of Philosophie.

The hieroglyphs are equated with the allegorical use of fables (as in Diodorus),
and both are assimilated to an evolving tradition of rhetoric and a moral art that
instructs by pleasing—a tradition that stretches in a not unduly complicated
way from the hieroglyphs to Sandys's latest publication. In this he resembles
the authors of the emblem books, who saw in the hieroglyphs a mode of
instruction even the illiterate could read—it is very different from the heremeti-
cists' conception of the hieroglyphs as an expression of a purer ancient knowledge deliberately hidden from the vulgar.

So for Sandys the hieroglyphs are less an object of mystic or occult knowledge than of historical knowledge (or historical scepticism)—and more a vehicle for moral meaning than either. For him the history of Egypt is not occult,
but simply unknown except in fragments. Egypt's cultural forms were widely
thought to be cryptic, either because the priests had veiled their wisdom from
the vulgar, or because (like the Muslims) they manipulated cultural forms for
their own nefarious ends. Both these ideas get into Sandys, but he is basically
sceptical. He does not try to write a secret history that will explain the Egyptian mysteries; his very neutrality leads him to try to construct a positive
cultural history, of necessity working backwards from Greece. In this his
approach is "progressive."

But if his humanism encourages him to take a critical attitude towards hermeticism, it also contains tendencies that work against what we think of as
properly historical thinking. As a good humanist, Sandys's conception of history was fundamentally rhetorical.[25] This had the effect in general of breaking
history down into a collection of *exempla*, usually moral ones. This tendency
was exacerbated in the case of Egypt by the absence of another strong historical
program (like the recovery of a valued civilization), which would anchor the
examples in a specific situation. It is further exacerbated by the fact that Egypt
is the home of the hieroglyphs. They keep asserting their presence as historical
artifacts on this leg of his journey, and as the meaning of Egypt precipitates
itself out into a collection of emblems and symbols, they often serve both as the
model for these formations and as the nucleus around which they form.

This is perhaps clearest when they are used to interpret nature, but the forms
of symbolism and interpretation associated with them are deeply embedded in
Sandys's presentation of ancient Egyptian history and culture, as we can see as
he takes us on a tour of the major monuments of ancient Egypt, describing each
in a set piece. These descriptions are developed enough to involve his imagination as well as his historical knowledge. The meanings he finds for the monuments are very different in kind; they all make extraordinary demands on his
sense of time and history, and he displays a whole range of responses, from
careful archaeological reconstruction to complete anachronism. The unsys-

tematic quality is a result of the shapelessness of Egyptian history, of the lack of a dominant historical myth; some coherence is brought to this array of responses by the tendencies to move in the direction of the classical and the emblematic.

As might be expected, the re-creation of "Alexandria when it flourished" is the most assured: it is of a piece with his handling elsewhere of classical civilization, and partakes of that myth.

> From the gate of the Sunne, vnto that of the Moone, on each side of the way stood ranks of pillars: in the middest a spacious Court, led into by a number of streets: in so much as the people that passed throughout, in some sort did seeme to haue vndertaken a iourney. On the left hand of this stood that part of the Citie which was named of *Alexander;* being as it were a City of it selfe, whose beauty did herein differ: for looke how farre those columnes directly extended in the former, so did they here, but obliquely placed. So that the sight dispersed through multitudes of waies, and rauished with the magnificency thereof, could hardly be satisfied. A wonderfull adorning hereunto were the Fanes, and regall pallaces, possessing welnigh a fourth part of the Citie; for euery one did striue to adde some ornament as well to the houses of their kings, as to the Temples of the Gods: which stood on the East side of the Citie; adioyning, and participating one with another. Amongst the which was that famous *Museum* founded by *Philadelphus,* & endowed with ample reuenues: planted with such as were eminent in liberall sciences, drawne thither by rewards, and cherished with fauours. [P. 111]

Sandys responds naturally and with sympathy to the brilliance of the Hellenistic city, which seems as solid and real as anything he sees with his own eyes. He still possesses a vision of the city, can remember what it looked like ("looke how farre . . . the sight dispersed . . . could hardly be satisfied"); the city still exists as a very concrete imaginative experience that has survived the passage of time, or rather has been recovered by the dedicated art and discipline of the Renaissance. There is a strong sense of a shared culture, of participation in a public space that is now literary, a cultural memory and ideal, but was once a physical reality on the spot where he now stands. The historical imagination displayed here is as vigorous as it is melancholy: this flourishing Alexandria is an illusion called up to illustrate again the "threatening instructions" of history, but the power of the vision remains even as Sandys moves with loving care through the familiar turn to the modern scene:

> Such was this Queene of Cities and Metropolis of *Africa:* but
>
> > Ah! how much different is
> > That Niobe from this!
> >
> > Ouid. Met. 1.6.
>
> who now hath nothing left her but ruines; and those ill witnesses of her perished beauties: declaring rather, that townes as well as men, haue their

ages and destinies. . . . Sundry mountaines are raised of the ruines, by
Christians not to be mounted; lest they should take too exact a survey of the
Citie: in which are often found (especially after a shower) rich stones, and
medals engrauen with the figures of their Gods, and men, with such perfec-
tion of art; as these now cut, seeme lame to those, and vnliuely counterfets.
[P. 114]

Sandys does not exaggerate the ruinous state of Alexandria he evokes so eloquently, though he ignores its immediate causes (a sharp decline in the spice
trade after the Portuguese voyages, and then the devastating Turkish invasion
of 1517). History has become an emblematic turn from an image of the past to
an image of the present, a transition with a moral: "Townes as well as men,
haue their ages and destinies." By the time the moral finds the life of man as its
center it has acquired a concentrated mass of references. The personification of
Alexandria elides the transition from men to town; town is an understated
abstraction of the vividly present (or vividly absent) Metropolis of Africa;
ancient Alexandria and its fall are, by an easy move, a synecdoche for all of
classical civilization and its fall. The learned detail and imaginative intensity of
Sandys's perception of all this illustrate the sublimity of history and thereby the
sublimity of loss as an element in man's moral life. Time is patterned into ages
and destinies, a tragic pattern.

The last of the ancient sites Sandys surveys is, like the first, a ruined city: like
Alexandria, Memphis becomes an emblem of the passage of time, but a starker,
more absolute one, because it is not contained within an historical memory
capable of restoring it.

Here also stood the Fane of *Venus*, and that of *Serapis*, beset with *Sphinxes*,
adioyning to the desert: a Citie great and populous, adorned with a world of
antiquities. But why spend I time about that that is not? The very ruines now
almost ruinated: yet some few impressions are left, and diuers throwne
downe, statues of monstrous resemblances: a scarce sufficient testimony to
shew vnto the curious seeker, that there it had bin. Why then deplore we our
humane frailty?

> When stones, as well as breath,
> And names do suffer death.
>
> *Auson.* [P. 132]

Memphis is a *memento mori.* The effort to know about it collapses under the
weight of an imponderable number of years, and so it produces an immediate
human significance, not an archaeological one. It exhausts the historian, recall-
ing his thoughts; because it is so remote it lets him stop where he is. He faces
the limits of historical knowledge, and it leads him to ask what should be taken
as a very real question about the point of venturing into history when it seems
to be only barren duration.

Perhaps the same exhaustion at the limits of historical knowledge explains the appeal of the mythological syncretism inherited from the Hellenistic age, and the unquestioning rapidity with which it is embraced—both the Virgilian account of burial customs and the syncretizing of Egyptian and Roman deities quoted earlier are grouped around this meditation on Memphis. The mind rebels at the proliferation of gods as at the extent of time; without the disciplines that make them manageable if infinite fields of knowledge, the mind throws off the burden at the first opportunity. The faster the gods collapse into one another and then into a transcendent principle, the better. If this syncretism "saves" the gods, it does not necessarily encourage interest in them. Sandys's imagination is not sent out to wander in the endless deserts of history and cultural complexity; it dwells in a classical, classicized Egypt where it is at least half at home. There it musters the energy to be interested in details, and to infuse spirit into its re-creations. It is only anachronism that keeps ancient Egypt from slipping away entirely.

The re-creation of the Labyrinth is of a very different kind. It too is converted into an experience, but that experience is a conventional moral allegory rather than a cultural memory or a meditation on the void.

> The passages thereunto through caues of maruelous length; full of winding paths as darke as hell, and roomes within one another, hauing many doores, to confound the memory, and distract the intention; leading into inexplicable errour, now mounting aloft, and againe redescending, not seldome turning about walls infolded within one another in the forme of intricate mazes, not possible to thred, or euer to get out without a conductor. The building more vnder the earth then aboue, being all of massie stone, and laid with that art, that neither cement nor wood was imployed throughout the vniuersall fabricke. The end at length attained to, a paire of staires of ninety steps conducted into a stately Portico supported with pillars of *Theban* stone: the entrance into a spacious hall (a place for their generall conuentions) all of polished marble, adorned with the statues of gods and men; with others of monstrous resemblances. The chambers were so disposed, that vpon their opening the doores did giue reports no lesse terrible then thunder. The first entrance was of white marble, within throughout adorned with marble columnes, and diuersitie of figures. By this defigured they the perplexed life of man: combred and intangled with manifold mischiefes, one succeeding another; through which vnpossible to passe without the conduct of wisdome, and exercise of vnfainting fortitude. [P. 113]

This passage depends on Pliny for its facts, but Pliny does not go nearly so far in rendering the Labyrinth as an experience—he is more interested in the floor plan that produces the effects.

> . . . passages that wind, advance, and retreat in a bewilderingly intricate manner. . . . doors are let into the walls at frequent intervals to suggest deceptively the way ahead, and to force the visitor to go back upon the very same tracks that he has already followed in his wanderings. . . . It is when he

is already exhausted with walking that the visitor reaches the bewildering maze of passages. . . . Some of the halls are laid out in such a way that when the doors open there is a terrifying rumble of thunder within: incidentally, most of the building has to be traversed in darkness.[26]

Sandys's rhetorical designs are very apparent in contrast to Pliny's off-handedness. Pliny's visitor actually distances us from the experience, reducing it to a tourist sight. The absent subject of Sandys's translation turns out to be nothing less than "the perplexed life of man," moved by labyrinthine syntax through a structure accommodated to its abstracted faculties ("to confound the memory, and distract the intention").

There is nothing in the ancient sources to authorize the notion that the purpose of the Labyrinth's design was allegorical, but that purpose is asserted ("By this defigured they the perplexed life of man"). For a Renaissance moralist the idea must have arisen inevitably from the architecture, and once the allegory has been located the whole description is beautifully recast as its vehicle. The Labyrinth becomes a pure idea, and if Pliny can lead us through it, Sandys can show us the way out ("through which vnpossible to passe without the conduct of wisdome, and exercise of vnfainting fortitude").

Once he has made his way through and then out of the allegory of the Labyrinth his interest in it is exhausted. It does not collapse, like the House of Busyrane, but it is lost or rather misplaced in Lake Mareotis near Alexandria, rather than in Lake Moeris above Memphis. This is the most serious geographical mistake in the *Relation.* More to our point, the Labyrinth has lost its cultural context, has become an ahistorical didactic *exemplum;* its meaning is assumed to be known, and does not need to be reconstructed or translated. Herodotus saw it as an overwhelming manifestation of Egyptian cultural power, and Pliny maintains a considerable critical distance ("We must mention also the labyrinths, quite the most abnormal achievement on which man has spent his resources, but by no means a fictitious one, as might well be supposed"). Sandys does not express either of these positions—as in the case of the hieroglyphs, once Egypt has put the symbol into circulation its concrete origins are forgotten and the fate of its ruins is not mentioned. Unlike the ruins of Alexandria and Memphis, the Labyrinth is an interpretative and rhetorical occasion divorced from history.

The Pyramids, on the other hand, were very much still there, thwarting an attempt to reduce them to an emblem of the ruins of time like Memphis. The Pharaohs built them in part

to giue vnto their fames eternity. But vainely:

> Not sumptuous Pyramis to skies vp-reard,
> Nor Elean Ioues proud Fane, which heauen compeered,
> Nor the rich fortune of Mausoleus tombe
> Are priuiledge'd from deaths extreamest doome.

> Or fire, or stormes, their glories do abate,
> Or by age shaken fall with their owne waight.
>
> Propert. 1.3 Eleg. 2

Yet this hath bene too great a morsell for time to deuoure; hauing stood, as may be probably coniectured, about three thousand and two hundred yeares: and now rather old then ruinous: yet the North side most worne, by reason of the humidity of the Northerne wind, which here is the moystest. The top at length we ascended with many pauses and much difficulty . . . [P. 129]

The embarrassed moralist becomes an archaeologist. (Sandys's description was the most thorough in English until John Greave's minor monument *Pyramidographia* [1646].)

But the physical description does not help to establish the meaning of the Pyramids; Sandys's inability to settle firmly on one meaning reflects uncertainty both about why they were built and about what the proper attitude towards them should be. His initial formula ("barbarous monuments of prodigality and vain-glory") is a mixture of echoes of Martial, who used the Pyramids as a standard of monumental fame *("Barbara pyramidum sileat miracula Memphis")*[27] and Pliny, who used them as a standard of monumental folly *("Dicantur obiter et pyramides in eadem Aegypto, regum pecuniae otiosa ac stulta ostentatio")*.[28]

The rest of the opening passage does not follow from either opinion:

> Full West of the Citie, close vpon those deserts, aloft on a rocky leuell adioyning to the valley, stands those three Pyramides (the barbarous monuments of prodigality and vain-glory) so vniuersally celebrated. The name is deriued from a flame of fire, in regard of their shape: broad below, and sharp aboue, like a pointed Diamond. By such the ancient did expresse the original of things, and that formlesse forme-taking substance. For as a Pyramis beginning at a point, and the principall height, by little and little dilateth into all parts: so Nature proceeding from one vndeuidable fountaine (euen God the soueraigne essence) receiueth diuersitie of formes; effused into seuerall kinds and multitudes of figures: vniting all in the supreme head, from whence all excellencies issue. [P. 127]

This is obviously anachronistic: the etymology is Greek, not Egyptian, and "the ancient" is a Neo-Platonist. These comments tend to increase the prestige of the Pyramids, but their relation to the actual masonry is very vague.

Various explanations are offered as to why the Pyramids were built. Following Pliny, Sandys suggests that their construction was a political strategy to employ the people and to exhaust corrupting excess wealth. "Besides, they considering the frailty of man, that in an instant buds, blowes, and withereth; did endeuour by such sumptuous and magnificent structures, in spite of death to giue vnto their fames eternity" (p. 129). And then:

They erecting such costly monuments, not onely out of a vaine ostentation: but being of opinion, that after the dissolution of the flesh the soule should suruiue; and when thirty six thousand yeares were expired, againe to be ioyned vnto the selfsame body, restored vnto his former condition: gathered in their conceipts from Astronomicall demonstrations. [Pp. 130–131]

The discussion of the Pyramids ends with a collection of legends linking their construction with prostitution—Cheops prostituted his daughters to pay for his, the smallest of the three was erected by or for a whore—unconfirmed rumours about which Sandys is sceptical, but they flavor his attitude towards the Pyramids. Perhaps the various elements in this collection of suggestions, explanations, and interpretations are not incompatible, but no attempt is made to outline a cultural matrix that would contain and reconcile them all. The meaning of the Pyramids is overdetermined, suggesting that there is a dynamic of forces working through the symbolic systems of Egyptian culture, which are not then absolute or univocal. But this richness of understanding of cultural motives is only partially realized: Sandys's position seems more incoherent than complex, its form the result of eclectic source-mining.

The case of the Sphinx is clearer and more acute. Sandys gives three distinct interpretations of it:

The vpper part of a *Sphinx* resembled a maide, and the lower a Lion; whereby the *AEgyptians* defigured the increase of the Riuer, (and consequently of their riches) then rising when the Sunne is in *Leo* and *Virgo*. . . . By a *Sphinx* the *AEgyptians* in their hieroglyphicks presented an harlot: hauing an amiable, and alluring face; but withall the tyrannie, and rapacity of a Lion: exercised ouer the poore heart-broken, and voluntarily perishing louer. The images of these they also erected before the entrances of their Temples; declaring that secrets of Philosophy, and sacred mysteries, should be folded in enigmaticall expressions, separated from the vnderstanding of the prophane multitude. [Pp. 131–32]

Now it seems that the Sphinx at Giza was a portrait statue of King Khafre (Chephren) of the 4th Dynasty, c. 2550 B.C., in the guise of the Sun god; it was restored in Dynasty 18 and was then identified with the Sun god Harmachis. Thereafter the sphinx as a visual motif migrated through the Levant to Greece, undergoing a sex change in the 14th century and acquiring wings. Its significance between the early Egyptian period and its reappearance in the Oedipus story is unclear. Meanwhile the statue with which we are concerned was buried by sand, not to be uncovered until the Ptolemaic period or even later, thereby rupturing the native tradition about it.[29]

Sandys, soon to become a professional mythographer, does not seem to notice a problem. He easily assimilates the Sphinx to three later iconographic traditions: the Zodiac (his source for this first interpretation is Belon, p. 117r); the monsters of which Scylla is the most famous example; and the late Greek riddling sphinx of the Oedipus story (cf. *Isis and Osiris,* 9: the Egyptians place "sphinxes before their shrines to indicate that their religious teaching has in it an enigmatical sort of wisdom").[30]

That the meanings produced by this anachronistic interpretation are incompatible with or at least unrelated to each other will not surprise anyone familiar with the ways of Renaissance mythographers, who were used to interpreting the same fable *in bono* and *in malo;* Sandys had made the Sphinx yield a meaning in the physical, moral, and mystical realms, which was the objective of his science. This agility of interpretation splinters the symbol in a way that makes it difficult to imagine the conditions of its original enunciation. Sandys simply asserts each time the integrity of the relation between symbol and meaning: "whereby the AEgyptians defigured," and so on.

He does not explain his theory of interpretation, but his assertion of an historical connection between symbol and meaning may itself be evidence that his theory of Egyptian symbols is not a Neo-Platonic, essentialist one. "Where symbols are believed not to be conventional but essential, their interpretation in itself must be left to inspiration and intuition," Gombrich says,[31] noticing that Ficino feels free to invent a new interpretation for one of Horapollo's hieroglyphs. The inspired contemplator is an authentic source of interpretations, and interpretation can go on indefinitely, expanding into all the forms in which his knowledge is organized (e.g. the physical, moral, and mystical). Bacon, working from very different assumptions, recovers a similar freedom to interpret by facing the historical problem of the relationship between myth and philosophy, and admitting his agnosticism. He recognizes how easily meanings can be inserted into fables which did not contain them, but:

> Upon the whole I conclude with this: the wisdom of the primitive ages was either great or lucky: great, if they knew what they were doing and invented the figure to shadow the meaning; lucky, if without meaning or intending it they fell upon matter which gives occasion to such worthy contemplations. My own pains, if there be any help in them, I shall think well bestowed either way: I shall be throwing light either upon antiquity or upon nature itself.[32]

Sandys's historical purposes interfere with any such freedom (or at least its admission)—he is only relaying received interpretations, which have historical authority. But how historical are his interpretations? To have undertaken the researches that would have shown that his received interpretations did not in fact originate with the Egyptians would have been an extraordinary project in an age that was just beginning to distinguish between original Egyptian hieroglyphs and its own inventions. It is hard to know how seriously he meant his assertions of the historical authenticity of his interpretations—one suspects he did not worry much about the risk of anachronism. His discipline provided him with meanings that are not unhappy, though they may be imperfectly historical. He did not have the resources of modern archaeology; if he had had its standards of interpretation he would not have been able to say anything at all about the Sphinx.

The form of his interpretation is probably more significant than the accuracy of its content. The three meanings he offers are still vital, but discontinuous with each other—they are anchored in one object, but are not mutually illuminating; all thought to be transmitted by history, but they are not related historically. In the same way that the Renaissance thought of the hieroglyphs as a collection of individual symbols rather than as a representation of a language with grammar and syntax, the Sphinx is a grab bag of symbolic meanings which are linked only in the simplest mode of accumulation, and which do not seem to emerge from any cultural process (except the Egyptian penchant for encoding, which is the mirror image of the interpreter's activity, and is again largely outside of history).[33] This is true in general of the representation of Egyptian culture and history—they are crystallized around a collection of objects and symbols, and this has the effect of atomizing them, of discouraging internal coherence. Emblematizing brings the object into a direct relation to the viewer's mind, but it tends to detach it from history, which tends then to be reduced to the medium in which the emblems are preserved. The Renaissance conception of the coherence of history and culture was founded in the study of language, but Egypt is not understood in relation to a normal language. The languages that are invoked are foreign, Greek and Latin, with the anachronistic effects that have been noticed.

5

The Holy Land

In the Holy Land Sandys gives constant evidence of his Protestantism by protesting against everything he is told about everything he sees. Devotion and tradition allow the pilgrim to abolish historical distance, but Sandys submits his tradition to historical criticism, and so he moves around in a state of sceptical alienation, entailing a constant stream of verbal qualifications:

An historian perhaps not alwaies to be credited. . . . so by them instild. . . . the *Iewes* do fable this place to haue bin. . . . (but with what congruity I know not). . . . this is said to haue hapned (though intermixed with fiction) about the time that. . . . But relations of that kind haue credit only in places far distant. . . . But our guides were well practiced in that precept: "of streames, Kings, fashions, kingdomes askt, there showne; / Answer to all: th'vnknowne relate as knowne" *Ouid,* who endeuour to bring all remarkable places within the compasse of their processions. The *Mahometans* either deceiued with this tradition, or maintaining the report for their profit. . . . whom I rather judge to haue bin buried at *Moden.* . . . This tradition how euer absurd, is generally belieued by those Christians: a place of high repute in their deuotions. . . . but not by my eyes apprehended. . . . as they would make vs beleeue. . . . But surely they be the eyes of faith that must apprehend it. . . . (so called of the inhabitants). . . . On the right hand in the court they vndertake to shew where the fire was made, by which Peter stood when he denied his Maister. . . . It is said to be about two miles long, and if it be so, but short ones. . . . Passing along we came to our Ladies fountaine (vpon what occasion they so call it, is not worth the relating). . . . they say. . . . they affirme. . . . (as they say). . . . the rest being such like stuff as the former, wherwith I haue already tired myselfe, and afflicted my Reader.

Such an attitude is antipathetic to devotional enthusiasm—in two instances only does religious experience break through Sandys's critical scepticism. The tone of this scepticism varies somewhat: on the excursion to Bethany Sandys is in a good mood, and we barely notice the endlessly repeated "they say"—it expresses a transparent guardedness that does not interfere with a constantly stimulated interest in this crowded landscape, with his pleasure in traversing this ground with all its memories. But on Easter Monday he rides out on the road to Emmaus, and doubts everything: he refuses to pay the excessive entrance fee to a tomb in which he cannot believe Samuel is buried; he does not participate in the devotions of the Friars who have accompanied him; he withholds himself and his belief, venting through his superior historical scholarship his boredom and irritation at what is being presented to him. He is in no mood for an apparition.

There was no way to escape the vexing patter of the Friars (who are the "they" of the formulaic and ubiquitous "they say"). The Turkish authorities delegated responsibility for all western Christians to the Franciscan Pater Guardian, and there was no place to stay in Jerusalem except in their monastery—one could not even get inside the city gates without their conduct. (In 1601 Henry Timberlake tried, standing on his identity as a Protestant and an Englishman, and refusing the protection of the Pater Guardian. The Turks said they had never heard of his country or his queen, and threw him into prison.)[1] Sandys found the Pater Guardian voluble and friendly, but he suspects the Franciscans of having murdered six Englishmen a few years earlier ("Seven they were in all, all alive and well one day, six dead in the other; the outliver becoming convert to their religion," p. 186). All sightseeing was done under the supervision of the Friars. Jean Zuallart explains how it went:

> Les deuotz pelerins & benings lectueurs, seront icy aduertis, qu'à ce sainct lieu & en tous les autres par nous visitez, le reuerend Pere Gardien ou autre conducteur des Pelerins en son lieu, nous fit des petites exhortations & recit, de ce qui estoit faict & representé en chacun: puis fut chanté en iceux le texte de l'Euangile ou autre partie de l'Escriture Saincte de ce faisant mention, & apres vne Antienne, & la collecte appropriée (comme verrez au dernier liure) auec vne declaration des graces & indulgences qu'on y acquiert pour tant plus attirer les coeurs des assistens à deuotion, & cest aduertissement seruira pour tout le rest.[2]

The whole experience was carefully controlled. An official certificate affirming that he had visited all the holy places was thrust on Sandys, as on all other visitors, by the Pater Guardian, in the course of his final fund-raising pitch. This certificate, the product of the same medieval Catholicism that sold indulgences, completes the reduction of the pilgrimage to a commodity, a process that began for most pilgrims with buying a package tour in Venice. Hakluyt prints the narrative of John Locke (1553) who simply substitutes such a certificate, in Latin, for an account of his travels once he arrives in the Holy Land.[3]

Thus the standardization of the pilgrims' movements (they all took the same series of excursions on the same schedule) was matched by an attempted standardization of experience. Zuallart, who gives a detailed account of all aspects of the pilgrimage, is also a fine example of the psychic power of the whole system. Even at its most mystical the experience was channeled into a form given in advance, the *imitatio Christi.*[4] Therefore pilgrimage narratives are not the place to look for personal impressions, for autobiography—the experience is not personal in that sense. The great majority of narratives take the form of simple testimonial, with no description and no response: "Then they shewed mee, the Church where the Virgin *Marie* fell into agony, when Christ passed by carrying his Cross."[5] One often feels a tremendous amount of pious emotion between the lines of these narratives, but their inarticulateness refers us to the institution that supports them. As early as the twelfth century personal narratives begin to repeat verbatim descriptions taken from guide books.[6]

The English Protestant traveler to the Holy Land always had to come to terms with this setup, which was more or less unacceptable and hostile to him. Timberlake reaches an accommodation with the Franciscans into whose custody he was released: when he is shown the place of Christ's Ascension on Mt. Olivet "At ye sight [t]hereof we said our prayers, and were commanded withall to say five *Pater Nosters,* & five *Ave Maries,* but we said the Lords prayer, took notice of the place and departed."[7] He is sometimes sceptical, but he is nevertheless a real pilgrim who falls down and prays when he first comes in sight of Jerusalem. What is wrong with the Holy Land is that the Muslims have ruined it, and he still relies on the structure of the Catholic pilgrimage to give his trip meaning:

> it is called *Terra Sancta* . . . bearing the name onley and no more: for all holiness is cleane banished from thence by those theeues, filthie Turks and Infidels that inhabite the same: And, hauing my certificate sealed by ye Guardian, and a letter deliuered vnto mee, to shew that I had washed my selfe in the Riuer of *Iordan,* I departed from *Ierusalem.* . . .[8]

Sandys dons a pilgrim's robes when he joins the caravan which brought him to Palestine from Cairo, and lets himself be carried along by the pilgrimage system, creating no disturbances—but he is distinctly not a pilgrim. As he approaches Jerusalem he is thinking about the myth of Perseus and Andromeda and its connection with Joppa, not preparing himself spiritually, and when the city comes into view his response is aesthetic, not devotional: "From hence to *Jerusalem* the way is indifferent even. On each side round hils, with ruines on their tops, the vallies, such as are figured in the most beautiful landskips" (p. 154). Instead of offering up prayers at the expected points he exercises his scepticism. In the Temple of Christ's Sepulcher

> After we had disposed of our luggage . . . the Confessor offered to shew vs the holy and obseruable places of the Temple: which we gladly accepted of; he demanding first if deuotion or curiosity had possest vs with that desire. So that for omitting *Pater nosters,* and *Aue Maries,* we lost many yeares indulgences, which euery place doth plentifully afford to such as affect them: and contented our selues with an historicall relation. [P. 163]

An historical relation here means scrupulous critical handling of the objects encountered on the pilgrim's path: throughout this book of the *Relation*, as in this passage, historical relation is in direct opposition to a devotional attitude, and to an easy access to the sacred. Jerusalem was "once sacred and glorious"—like glory, holiness passes away in time, leaving behind relics that are empty. Sandys's attitude is radically informed by the Protestant objections to idolatry, to superstition, to confusing the spiritual with the material. The very conjunction of the words "Holy" and "Land" makes him uneasy: he goes out of his way to tell us this is the Crusaders' phrase, not his (p. 145),[9] and he distances himself from the belief of the Christians living there, who "impute to the place an adherent holinesse" (p. 146).

Samuel Purchas, who included this part of Sandys's *Relation* in *Purchas his Pilgrimes*, is an appropriate source for theological commentary on Sandys's attitude—he makes endlessly explicit what is usually implicit in Sandys. His choice of titles for his two books *(His Pilgrimage, then His Pilgrimes)* led him to explain time and again that the notion of pilgrimage should always be taken metaphorically. So when Sandys has one of his rare outbursts of Crusading rage against the infidels who now regulate the institutions of pilgrimage—"O who can without sorrow, without indignation behold the enemies of Christ to be the Lords of his Sepulcher!"—Purchas corrects him with a note:

> Let his friends enjoy him, and Heaven where is his glory: as for his Sepulcher, He is risen, he is not there. And what have his enemies, but what himselfe would not hold, and which could not hold him? Which it hath pleased him to permit to them, that his followers might follow him to heaven in their affections and conversation, Col.3. Phil.3.. . . . Pilgrimages are good, when we are thereby made Pilgrimes from the world and our selves. Thy selfe is the holyest place thou canst visit, if with faith and repentance made the Lords Temple, which the Jewish signified. . . .[10]

Purchas's allegory undercuts sacred geography by finding that its center no longer occupies literal geographical space: "He is risen, he is not there." Geography then becomes meaningless, strictly speaking, from a religious point of view: devotion is entirely individual and internal. But the coming and then going of the divine through Palestine has left it visibly traumatized. Elsewhere Purchas, disgusted by the contemporary population of Palestine, reverses the dominant geographical trope of Christendom, calling the Holy Land the "Knave-ill" of the world, the center to which refuse sinks (8:76).

Likewise Sandys's brief history of the Holy Land emphasizes ruptures with the sacred rather than continuities. This is a land wasted by divine vengeance, not a land of promission. The Old and New Testament histories are summarized in very abbreviated form, doubtless because they were too familiar to bear repetition; nevertheless the impression created is that history leads not towards Christ as the fulfillment of a typological scheme, but away from him.

"But the calamities of that warre inflicted by *Gallus, Vespasian,* and *Titus,* exceeded both example, and description. *His bloud be on us and ours:* a wish then granted, was now effected with all fulnesse of terrour" (pp. 144–45). And then:

> A countrey it seemeth anathemated, for the death of Christ, and slaughter of so many Saints: as may be conceiued by view of the place itselfe; and ill successe of the Christian armies: which in attempting to recouer it haue endured there so often such fatall ouerthrowes: or else, in reputing it a meritorious warre, they haue prouoked the diuine vengeance. [P. 145]

The world is unredeemable, and it is wrong even to try to introduce the divine into the confusions of history. Like the Chosen People, the Promised Land is not sanctified by the intervention of the divine, but especially damned for its unworthiness. It is typical of Sandys to come down on this end of the historical process—what needs to be explained is devastation, and the Holy Land offers the simplest and most terrible example of guilt and retribution.

Sandys is caught between two mythic visions. In one of them Palestine labors under a dark curse, is "anathemated," is to be contemplated with horror; in the other it is really a Holy Land. These two visions interfere with each other, each keeping the other from gaining ascendancy. Out of their interference comes Sandys's objective and historical treatment of Palestine, which permits him to avoid making a choice. He will still use the name "The Holy Land," but under protest, holding it at a philological distance. The meaning of the Holy Land is that it once had a sacred meaning which has withdrawn. One does not make a pilgrimage to such a place, but the idea creates the appropriate position from which to examine relics that have been incorporated into a system that falsifies their meaning—it is a theory of the inadequacy, the poverty, of the signs obtruded on the pilgrim. The mendacious accretions of Catholic tradition fill a vacuum left by an awesome loss.

So, to choose an example more or less at random, Sandys is led into a

> Church dedicated to the blessed Angels, and belonging to the *Armenians,* who haue their dwellings about it. Within the court there is an old oliue tree, enuironed with a low wall; vnto which, it is said, that they bound our Sauiour. Turning on the right hand, we went out at the port of *Sion.* [p. 185]

The meaning of this event in the Passion is totally incommensurate with the shabby, worn-out tree to which it has been attached by tradition, and Sandys does nothing to bring them together—everything about his tone drives them further apart. He is not a preacher expounding on the spiritual meaning of the event, which was so intimately familiar to his audience that appropriating it on his authority as a mere traveler would be insolent. Nor is he an historian imaginatively re-creating the past. Ancient Jerusalem is re-created for us, but on the whole there is less historical re-creation in this part of the *Relation* than anywhere else, probably in part because the events of the New Testament are not importantly related to architecture, the material with which Sandys was used to working. What was always venerated was the *spot*, not what had originally been built on it; the case of Alexandria, for instance, is completely different.

Moreover, to re-create the events that give the spot its meaning would be to transgress into the realm of the spiritual exercise of the composition of place. Pilgrims were coached in this exercise: Zuallart repeats a long speech made by the Pater Guardian to the newly arrived pilgrims, touching on (among other topics) the way the Holy Sepulcher was to be approached:

> toutes les fois qu'y entrons en contemplation, nous y voyons le Sauueur couché, enueloppé de linges, & y demeurant quelque peu, les Anges seoir à ses pieds, & le suarie gisant au chef, luy estant glorieusement resuscité. En ce S. lieu, auec la Mere, pouuons plorer & estre ioieux. . . .[11]

But Zuallart's own account does not read like this: like many other pilgrims he repeats the story whose setting he is visiting, but he does not pretend to re-create it, to make it over in his imagination. We learn what prayers he said, and something about how he felt, but what he tells us (he repeats most of what the guide told him, and more: he can give a lengthy commentary, with bibliography, on nearly every stone) is preparatory to this sort of heightened dramatic enactment, which is left to his reader's imagination. Such was the proper role of the travel writer.[12]

These spiritual exercises were well known in England[13] but they were viewed with suspicion in some circles. Sandys's reticence in giving free rein to his historical imagination is probably due to the sort of anxiety that Thomas Fuller faces—sometimes with irony—at the beginning of *A Pisgah-sight of Palestine.* Again and again Fuller feels compelled to explain that his labors are designed solely to be "Usefull . . . for the understanding of the Scriptures," and not for any more questionable purposes.

> It matters not to any mans salvation, to know the accurate distance betwixt *Jericho* and *Jerusalem;* and he that hath climbed to the top of mount *Libanus,* is not in respect of his soul, a haires breadth nearer to heaven. Besides, some conceive they heare *Palestine* saying unto them, as *Samuel* did to *Saul* endevouring to raise him from his grave, *Why hast thou disquieted me to bring me up?* Describing this Countrey is but disturbing it, it being better to let it sleep quietly, intombed in its owne ashes. The rather, because the *New Jerusalem* is now daily expected to come down, and these corporall (not to say carnall) studies of this terrestriall *Canaan,* begin to grow out of fashion, with the more knowing sort of Christians.
>
> 6. It is answered, though these studies are not essentiall to salvation, yet they are ornamentall, to accomplish men with knowledge, contributing much to the true understanding of the History of the Bible. . . .

Our work in hand is a parcell of Geography touching a particular description of *Judea;* without some competent skill wherein, as the blind *Syrians* intending to go to *Dothan,* went to *Sameria;* so ignorant persons discoursing of the Scripture, must needs make many absurd, and dangerous mistakes. . . .

7. But this last objection being forked, hath the sharper point thereof still behind, challenging this our subject to be guilty of superstition. . . . Sure if this our work were faulty in this kind, I my self would send it the same way with the *Ephesian conjuring books.* . . . wherein studiously we have abstained from all such pictures as come within the bounds of danger, yea borders of offence, and have onely made choice of those, which the most precise approve usefull for the illustration of Scripture.[14]

That a geographer should be so worried about this problem is remarkable; the traveller would have to feel it even more acutely. So although elsewhere Sandys feels free to use imaginative methods of interpretation and re-creation to develop the meaning of the past, here they are displaced by their more potent religious equivalents, to which the *Relation* becomes a humble handmaiden with strictly limited aims.

Nor, finally, is the meaning of the event projected inward, into his personal spiritual life. The narrative follows Sandys about, but it does not follow the motions of his interior life, except very intermittently, or through the subtle shadings of his tone. In the Temple of Christ's Sepulcher he tells us that his description will follow the floor plan, not the order in which things were shown him; he also implicitly rejects the historical, dramatic order of the Stations of the Cross, though he watched a procession following that order. The form he works in is the survey. This ceaseless attention to objects and the arbitrariness with which they are brought to his attention interfere with both a reconstitution of the historical events and a narrative of spiritual experience. Those potentialities are imprisoned in the travel narrative and the objects given to it. Subject and object reach their limits of contraction, with the intended result of a more or less scientific description—detached, cool, critical—of what was there to be seen and touched. Places, the memorials and dead husks of spiritual events, are given to the travel writer to handle, but they are all that is to be found in the Holy Land anyway.

Because this part of the *Relation* is so oriented around the description of shrines, the historical figures who bulk largest in it are (after Christ himself) the great builders of churches, St. Jerome's protégée, the noble Roman Paula, and Constantine's mother, "the vertuous *Helena* (of whom our country may iustly glorie)." They represent as well the intersection of Christianity with the classical world, and the resulting institutionalization of Christianity. Sandys is opposed to the accretions of Catholic legend, but not to institutionalization (his father was an archbishop). He clearly admires these great ladies and the splendid scale of their piety, and is in sympathy with their work. The decay or destruction of their churches is a familiar theme, more approachable and more often stated than the encompassing historical myth of Christ's revelation and the divine vengeance wreaked upon Israel. The shrines have an interest independent of their connection with Christ; even if they fail to mediate the meaning of Christ's life for Sandys, they are worth talking about as cultural artifacts. He is apparently not stirred religiously by visiting the church St. Helena built over Christ's supposed birthplace in Bethlehem, but he clearly thinks building the church was a reasonable thing to do, and he has some faith in the authenticity of the location. He appreciated it as an aesthetic accomplishment:

> the sides . . . are vpheld with foure ranks of pillars (ten in a row) each of one entire marble: white, and in many places beautifully speckled: the largest, and fairest that euer I saw: whose vpper ends do declare that they haue in part bene exquisitely guilded. . . . lamps still burning do expell the naturall darknesse; and giue a greater state thereunto then the light of the day could affoord it. [Pp. 177, 181]

Helena's church is the noblest expression of the institution of pilgrimage, but Sandys's interest extends to the more degraded aspects of the institution as well. The miserable villagers outside "who get a beggarly liuing by selling vnto strangers the models of the Sepulcher, and of the Grot of the Natiuitie; cut in wood or cast in stone, with crosses, and such like merchandizes" are also part of the meaning of the site. The coolly detached registering of the shabbiness, of the meaningless souvenirs, of the very failure to move him, attests again to an attitude towards history that is the opposite of the pilgrim's. The original event is no longer there in any significant way; its significance has drained away, has been betrayed, is never fully brought into play. What is left is a mere institution, to be approached in merely sociological or historical or aesthetic terms.

Sandys's whole report on the Holy Land is remarkable for the extent to which the expression of faith is suppressed. The objectivity of his description is the direct result of this suppression, of his success in keeping that question from interfering with his orderly procedures. In his apology for adding another account of Jerusalem to the heap he promises

> to deliuer the Reader from many erring reports of the too credulous deuoute, and too too vain-glorious: the one
>
> Do toyes diuulge——

The other charactered in the remainder of that Disticke:

> ——Still adde to what they heare,
And of a mole-hill do a mountaine reare.
>
> Bapt. Mant. 1.3.

I will declare what I haue obserued, vnswayed with either of their vices. [P. 154]

Another vice he is unswayed by is that of the Protestants who, if they did not succumb to the temptations of credulity (as many did), gave vent to their faith in violent, often nearly blasphemous opposition to everything around them. Sandys's unremitting but steady scepticism is an emotional as well as rhetorical achievement.

Though his religious emotions are almost entirely unspoken, Sandys clearly had faith and expected his readers to share it. The problem that concerned him was where to place his faith, his fear that it would be misplaced and so defiled. Only twice does he permit himself to be overwhelmed with religious emotion, to give a positive expression to his faith, and then only when his obsessive concern with historical authenticity, and his doubts about the sanctity of places, can be satisfied or at least mooted. On both occasions he is within the Temple of Christ's Sepulcher in Jerusalem, already at the center of Christendom.

> At the East end vnder a large arched concaue of the wall, is the place whereon our Sauiour did suffer, and may assuredly be thought the same: and if one place be more holy then another reputed of, in the world the most venerable. He is void of sence that sees, beleeues, and is not then confounded with his passions. [P. 164]

The exact nature of the experience, or of the holiness of the place, is not quite clear. The sequential construction ("sees, beleeues, and . . . then") suggests that the experience of holiness is not of a numinous presence, but of an especially intense act of believing. This belief is historical, and never gets completely free from the problems of historical belief. His resistance gives way, but it is so ingrained that the positive expression takes the form of a negation of a negation, hedged around with qualifications and assurances. We get not a realized identity of pilgrim with Christ but an attack on a straw man who is not confounded with his passions, which looks like an attempt by Sandys to wrench himself out of the posture maintained everywhere else in the *Relation*.

Sandys's religion encouraged him to make distinctions, to be careful, to withhold himself, to purify his belief—it supports all his historical criticism, and probably inhibits the expression of his passion. His religious experience is immediately circumscribed, strictly localized; it is also strictly individual. There is no feeling of community, either existential or historical, with his fellow Christians.[15] They are a colorful lot, but they seem nearly as alien as the Muslims. Sandys's passion is set off by a satiric description of what "they", the pilgrims, do: the boundary of the sacred and the pure is emphasized by introducing the profane and the vulgar.

> This place is too holy to be trod vpon. They weare the hard stones with their soft knees, and heate them with their feruent kisses; prostrating themselues, and tumbling vp and downe with such an ouer-actiue zeale, that a faire *Greeke* virgine, ere aware, one morning shewed more then intended: who

the Frier that helpt the Priest to say Masse so tooke at the bound, that it ecchoed againe, and disturbed the mournefull sacrifice with a mirthfull clamour; the poore maid departing with great indignation. [P. 165]

The only time Sandys appears to feel a sesne of brotherhood is under the pressure of a still stronger experience at the edge of Christ's Sepulcher itself.

Thousands of Christians performe their vowes, and offer their teares here yearely, with all the expressions of sorrow, humilitie, affection, and penitence. It is a frozen zeal that will not be warmed with the sight thereof. And o that I could retaine the effects that it wrought, with an vnfainting perseuerance! who then did dictate this hymne to my Redeemer:

> Sauiour of mankind, Man, Emmanuel:
> Who sin-lesse died for sinne, who vanquisht hell.
> The first fruites of the graue. Whose life did give
> Light to our darknesse: in whose death we liue.
> O strengthen thou my faith; correct my will,
> That mine may thine obey: protect me still.
> So that the latter death may not deuoure
> My soule seal'd with thy seale. So in the houre
> When thou whose Body sanctifide this Tombe,
> Vniustly iudg'd, a glorious Iudge shalt come
> To iudge the world with iustice; by that signe
> I may be knowne, and entertaind for thine. [P. 167]

One might suspect, ungraciously, that Sandys's feeling of at-oneness with the other Christians is related to the physical design of the Chapel of the Sepulcher: the pretty pilgrim and ribald Friar play out their profane little drama within a few feet of where the Cross stood, but the Chapel of the Sepulcher is so small that no more than three persons can enter it at once. The Christian community can only be an idea there, not a disturbing physical presence.

The spontaneous composition of a hymn is itself a Protestant declaration of spiritual autonomy, in contrast to the prepared prayers Catholic pilgrims were instructed to repeat at every step. Yet there is a curious impersonality and lack of a certain kind of immediacy about this whole passage, in spite of its obvious intensity and sincerity. Once again we have the straw man of the frozen zeal; and we are never quite told what are the effects the experience wrought. Sandys immediately worries that the experience will be endangered by time, the familiar problem of the perseverance of the spiritual in history, this time his personal history. There is no narrative here, and so we have to guess at the experience. The prayer concerns an alignment of his will in a set of abstract relations; it implicates a spiritual future rather than an autobiographical past. Its poetic effects are based on play with these abstractions (death, justice, etc.), and the absoluteness of the terms discourages the imagination. The power of his impulse derives from contact with this most sacred of places, but the power of the poem does not—very little is made of the dramatic setting within the poem, which is almost completely purified of experience, of the presentness of the Sepulcher itself. The concrete space and time Sandys has so laboriously traversed and then represented in his traveling and travailing are not drawn into the poem (as they are in his later autobiographical poem "Deo Opt. Max.", where the composition of this hymn is seen as the central event in his life; v. Chapter 2). His care to avoid any suggestion of a pilgrimage is a way of defusing the psychic pressures that must have been engendered by standing on what might be holy ground in a pilgrim's costume, surrounded by an atmosphere of deep (perhaps hysterical) devotion. Some distance from this atmosphere is the necessary condition for a measured Protestant response.

Sandys's classicism also helps to create some distance from everything associated with the pilgrimage—including specifically Protestant reactions. It is much less evident and much less programmatic than in the sections of the *Relation* dealing with Egypt and Italy; often it seems to float to the surface unintentionally, as a natural consequence of its entrenched position in Sandys's style and personality. It is not always perfectly integrated with his Christian faith, but its very extraneousness fleshes out his identity; and the presence of two competing patterns of perception solidifies the external reality. We are perhaps most apt to feel the incongruity in his classicism when it seizes control of his sensibility at awkward moments. An example is his appeal to Juvenal as he criticizes the way Mt. Calvary has been built over

> so that those naturall formes are vtterly deformed, which would haue better satisfied the beholder; and too much regard hath made them lesse regardable. For as the Satyre speaketh of the fountaine of *AEgera*,
>
> > How much more venerable had it beene,
> > If grasse had cloth'd the circling banks in greene,
> > Nor marble had the natiue tophis marr'd. [P. 161]

In this case the effect is a little shocking: that he should appeal to pagan aestheticism rather than to a Protestant argument at this moment makes one doubt his loyalties. His impression of John the Baptist's cave in the wilderness ("A place that would make solitarinesse delightfull, and stand in comparison with the turbulent pompe of cities," p. 183) is less overt but still unmistakable. This sentence serves very well to indicate why Sandys enjoyed his picnic there, but pastoral dreams can only falsify the life of John the Baptist, and so the traveler seems to be out of tune with the landscape and his mission in it as pilgrim or anti-pilgrim.

On other levels his classicism is legitimized by the historical intervention of the Greeks and Romans (Western and then Eastern) into the Holy Land, redrawing its map.[16] Sandys is as usual suave and flexible in following the multileveled mappings of this territory, from the Old Testament configurations through the Roman administrative units and the ecclesiastical jurisdictions of the early Church, to the Crusader kingdom and the current political organization under the Turks. But the classical Levant stands out with particular clarity. It has already been noticed that the coast figures in an Ovidian world, and that the cultural and institutional intersection of Rome and Christianity arouses special interest in the works of Paula and Helena. The formal historical narrative shows an even more striking intrusion of the classical world.

Sandys's formal history of the Holy Land is a secular political history, not a religious history tracing the evolution of Judaism or reflecting a Judeo-Christian historical scheme. The very abbreviated summary of the Old Testament begins to expand only with the Maccabees, who are handled not as actors in a religious drama but as examples of heroic patriotic virtue—a model whose inspiration looks very Roman.

> To oppose this tempest vp stood *Mathias* a Priest of the race of *Asmones,* with his fiue sonnes; all men of incomparable valour. Of whom *Iudas Maccabeus,* did (if not restore) vphold their State from a farther declination. *Iudas* slaine, *Iohn* succeeded him: *Ionathan, Iohn;* and *Simon, Ionathan,* the last of the breathren, (for *Eleazer* was slaine before by the fall of an Elephant which he slue, supposing it to haue borne the person of *Antiochus:*) all dying nobly in their countries defence; a glorious and to be emulated destiny. [P. 143]

The tangled story of the later Maccabees and the consolidation of Roman power is recorded in altogether disproportionate detail: this brief period is given as much space as the entire history up until that point. Of course this was the immediate political context into which Christ was born, but that is not emphasized; the apparent intersection is with classical history and historiography, not with divine history. Christ himself is introduced in a subordinate clause.

> *Archelaus* banished soone after for his cruelty, did die in exile, his *Ethnarchy* reduced into a *Romane* Prouince, and the gouernment therof committed vnto *Pontius Pilate* by *Tyberius Caesar:* vnder whom the Sonne of God did die for the offences of Man: foretold by heathen Oracles.
>
> > But when with hands out-stretcht, and head thorne-bound;
> > A cursed speare his blessed side shall wound:
> > For which abortiue night for three houres space
> > Shall mid-day maske. To mans affrighted race
> > The Temple then shall yeeld a dire ostent,
> > He shall to profound hell make his descent,
> > And shew the dead a way to life——
> >
> > *Siby, Orac.* 1.1.

His name thus couertly expressed

> Foure vowels hath it, and two that are none,
> Of Angels two: the summe of all thus shone.
> Eight monads, decads eight, eight hecatons
> Declare his name to earths vnfaithful sonnes.
>
> *Siby. Orac. 1.1.* [P. 144]

Heathen oracles are substituted for a Judaic typological foreshadowing, of which we hear nothing. In fact this passage stands in for the whole of the New Testament: the political narrative immediately resumes ("*Petronius* succeeded *Pilate; Felix, Petronius:* then *Festus, Albinus,* and *Florus. Florus* his cruelty and bad gouernment prouoked the Iewes to rebellion.") Christ and Christianity are as invisible to this narrative as they would have been to a contemporary Roman historian. Christ reappears only as the cause of the vengeance wreaked by God through the agency of the Romans, and the Christians reappear only in the reign of Constantine.

The holiness of the Holy Land is stated at the head of this narrative, with the help of an unidentified poem:

This famous countrey, the stage of wonders

> Loued of God; planted by first Colonies:
> Nurse of blest Saints; and kingly Families;
> Fruitfull in Worthies, glorious in the birth
> Of Christ: who here descending from the skies,
> Did with his bloud purge the polluted earth. . . . [P. 142]

but this significance is not realized in the narrative, just as all the memorials of Christ's life are not quickened by the presence of a living Jesus.

At these moments we feel the unresolved conflict in Renaissance culture between its classical and Christian elements, here manifesting itself as a sort of generic inertia: the classical elements in the rest of the *Relation* generate enough momentum so that, coupled with the religious inhibitions discussed above, they interfere with the articulation of a purely Christian experience of the Holy Land. Travelers across this terrain had been wandering and going astray for centuries: the pilgrim Sir John Mandeville (14th century) is distracted by a variety of pagan marvels; the pilgrim Jean Zuallart (1607) rather unwillingly brings Ovid and Virgil and others into a late edition of his *Le Tres-devot Voyage de Ierusalem,* "m'estant efforcé de rechercher les escripts de quelques Ethniques, pour en partie satisfaire aux honeurs d'aucuns de ce siecle malheureux, qui adiousteront plustost foy à ceux là, qu'aux escripts des saincts peres" ("Au lecteur"). Still this conflict, unresolved though it may be, creates a problematic of representation which is actually quite stable; one does not feel that Sandys's soul was wracked by the tension between his love of Ovid and his Anglicanism either.

The coherence of the representation of the Holy Land is very apparent as Sandys leaves it, riding north into the ancient territory of Phoenicia—a movement that eventually leads to the epistemological jumble at the end of the Third Book that we discussed in Chapter 2. On the whole Phoenicia is considered as a fringe of the classical world rather than as a source of abominations for the Hebrews. The glory of Tyre "is described by Ezechiel, and destruction foretold" prophetically, but Sandys is much more interested in the later siege by Alexander, "whose vndefatigable perseuerance made all things possible" (p. 214). Sidon may have been built by Sida the daughter of Belus, of Jovian lineage, or by Sidon the firstborn of Canaan; or its name may be derived from the Phoenician word for fish (p. 210). We can admire the pressure exercised on this question from so many angles at once by his learning, but the results are inconclusive. Phoenicia is handled like a miniature Egypt: special attention is paid to its relations with, and legacy to, other powers in the ancient world. Important topics are its cultural inventions and its colonies under Cadmus and Dido. But the ancients simply knew much less about it than about Egypt, and no imposing monuments remained to guide the imagination. Sandys knows Appian's and Ausonius's objections to Virgil's Dido, interfering with the adoption of that major literary resource. Unlike Egypt Phoenicia did not inspire strong feelings; there were no powerful motives or motifs informing its representation. This combined with lack of materials and its relative unimportance keeps ancient Phoenicia from emerging with much actuality, and prevents it from attaining hegemony over the representation of its ancient territories.

All kinds of influences penetrate the resulting vacuum. The myth of the Golden Age, which seems to lurk in the wings of every Renaissance imagination, arbitrarily takes up residence in some caves until the first historical occupants arrive.

Beyond on the left hand of the way are a number of Caues cut out of the rock, the habitations, as I suppose, of men in the Golden Age, and before the foundation of Cities.

When coole caues humble dwelling did affoord.
The fire, Lar, cattell, with their honours plac't
All vnder one shed: when the wife then chast
(For then vncourtly) made her siluan bed
Of straw, and leaues, with skinnes of wilde beasts spred.

Juue. Sat.6

These are mentioned in the booke of *Iosua*, and called *Mearah* (which is, the caues of the Sidonians), and afterward called the caues of *Tyrus*, a place then inexpugnable, and maintained by the Christians, vntill in the yeare 1167, it was by the corrupted souldiers deliuered to the *Saracens*. [P. 213]

Just before the caves Sandys passes a mosque "erected, as they say, ouer the widowes house that entertained *Elias*"; and on the other side of a valley he comes to an hospitable village,

> the same by all likelihood that was formerly called *Palaetyrus*, or old *Tyrus*. Forget I must not the custome obserued by the inhabitants hereabout, who retaine the old worlds hospitality. Be the passenger Christian or whatsoeuer, they will house him, prepare him extraordinary fare, and looke to his Mule, without taking of one Asper. But these precise *Mahometans* will neither eate nor drinke with a Christian: onely minister to his wants; and when he hath done, breake the earthen dishes wherein he hath fed, as defiled. [P. 214]

The same warmth suffuses this little corner of the landscape over the ages, but all the historical connections are missing—the specious coherence turns out to be nothing but a coincidence. The fact that the Golden Age lives on does not, paradoxically, made it more approachable. Though Sandys enjoys its hospitality he is excluded from the society itself by a system of taboos not mentioned in the literary sources, and this sours the whole exchange. They may have the old world's virtues, but they are after all Mahometans.

The confused and difficult history and topography of the Lebanon encourages these vestigial pockets of resistance to the major systems operating in the Levant—Muslim hegemony and the orbit of the Judeo-Christian Holy Land.

> The inhabitants are of sundry Nations and religions; gouerned by a succession of Princes, whom they call *Emers:* descended, as they say, from the *Druses,* the remainder of those French men which were brought into these parts by *Godfrey* of *Bullen:* who driuen into the mountaines aboue, and defending themselues by the aduantage of the place, could neuer be vtterly destroyed by the *Saracens.* At length they afforded them peace, and libertie of religion; conditionally that they wore the white Turbant, and paid such duties as the natural subject. But in tract of time they fell from the knowledge of Christ: nor throughly embracing the other, are indeed of neither. [P. 210]

Sandys is wrong about the Druses' religion, but he is right about the political implications of the terrain. As for the current Emir:

> he was neuer knowne to pray, nor euer seene in a Mosque. His name is *Faccardine*, small of stature, but great in courage and atchieuements: about the age of forty, subtill as a foxe, and not a little inclining to the Tyrant. He neuer commenceth battell, nor executeth any notable designe, without the consent of his mother.
>
> > Skill'd in blacke Arts, she makes streams backward runne:
> > The vertues knowes of weeds; of laces spunne
> > On wheeles; and poison of a lust-stung mare.
> > Faire dayes makes cloudie, and the cloudie faire:

Starres to drop bloud; the Moone looke bloudily;
And plum'd (aliue) doth through nights shadows fly.
The dead cals from their graues to further harmes:
And cleaues the solid earth with her long charmes.

Ouid. Amo. 1.1. E1.8 [Pp. 210–11]

The Emir is an exotic character, and his mother is an incarnation of the exotic, a
Medean witch who for thousands of years has been exercising her dark powers
in the same place—at the edge of the European psyche—whether that place is
called Colchis or Carthage or, this time, Sidon.

We hear a great deal about the career of this Emir, who was in more or less
open revolt against his Turkish overlord. It is an occasion for a view of how the
Turkish Empire worked, or did not work. This was not a disinterested question.

> The *Grand Signior* doth often threaten his subuersion: which he puts off
> with a iest, that he knowes he will not this yeare trouble him: whose displea-
> sure is not so much prouoked by his incroching, as by the reuealed intelli-
> gence which he holds with the *Florentine;* whom he suffers to harbor within
> his hauen of *Tyrus* (yet excusing it as a place lying waste, and not to be
> defended) to come ashore for fresh-water, buyes of him vnderhand his
> prizes, and furnisheth him with necessaries. But designes of a higher nature
> haue bene treated of betweene them, as is well knowne to certaine merchants
> imployed in that businesse. And I am verily perswaded, that if the occasion
> were layd hold of, and freely pursued by the Christians, it would terribly
> shake if not vtterly confound the *Ottoman* Empire. [P. 212]

This is not the nostalgic dream of a Crusader hoping for the reestablishment of
a Christian kingdom in the Holy Land: it is a glimmer in the eye of a proto-
imperialist, looking forward to a new mapping of this territory that would not
be carried through for years to come.

The merchants trading in the Emir's domain were mostly English, as we
learn on the same page, and they were increasingly concerned about the conditions under which they had to operate. Sandys, whose family was heavily
involved with the trading Companies, and who spent most of his time in the
Levant in the company of English merchants, was very alive to their concerns.
The long discussion of the long-defunct Tyrian purple dye industry, to take one
example, is perhaps not so strictly antiquarian as it seems: blue dye figures
largely in a document entitled "A briefe Remembrance of things to be inde-
voured at Constantinople, and in other places in Turkie, touching our Clothing
and our Dying, and things that bee incident to the same, and touching ample
vent of our naturall commodities, & of the labour of our poore people withall,
and of the generall enriching of this Realme: drawn by M. Richard Hakluyt of
the middle Temple, and given to a friend that was sent into Turkie 1582."[17]

Sandys's historical sense of the Levant includes the present scene, and the potentialities of the future, in the context of secular power. The Levant appeared to be penetrable by English interests and English power, and this aspect of his relation to the landscape also helps to determine how he sees it. He says that the Holy Land is "A countrey it seemeth anathemated, for the death of Christ, and slaughter of so many Saints: as many be conceiued by view of the place it selfe," but as he rides through it he seems to see not signs of divine vengeance but an underdeveloped country, a mismanaged agriculture, a stagnant economy.

> For [the Christians] here do liue in a subiection to be pitied; not so much as daring to hauc handsome houses, or to imploy their grounds to the most benefit. So dangerous it is to be esteemed wealthy. [P. 150]

> We past this day through the most pregnant and pleasant vally that euer eye beheld. On the right hand a ridge of high mountaines, (whereon stands *Hebron*): on the left hand the *Mediterranean* sea, bordered with continued hills, beset with variety of fruites: as they are for the most part of this dayes iourney. The champion between about twenty miles ouer full of flowry hils ascending leasurely, and not much surmounting their rancker valleys: with groues of oliues, and other fruites dispersedly adorned. Yet is this wealthy bottom (as are all the rest) for the most part vninhabited, but onely for a few small and contemptible villages, possessed by barbarous *Moores;* who till no more then will serue to feede them: the grasse wast-high, vnmowed, vneaten, and vselessly withering. [P. 151]

> The countrey such (but that without trees) as we past through before. No part so barren, but would proue most proffitable, if planted with vines, and fruites. . . . [P. 152]

> . . . aspiring mountaines; whereof some are cut (or naturally so) in degrees like allies, which would be else vnaccessably fruitlesse, whose leuels yet beare the stumps of decayed vines, shadowed not rarely with oliues and locusts. And surely I thinke that all or most of these mountaines haue bin so husbanded, else could this little country neuer haue sustained such a multitude of people. [P. 183]

> But now returne we to the summit of mount *Oliuet,* which ouertoppeth the neighbouring mountaines, whose West side doth giue you a full suruey of each particular part of the City: bedect with Oliues, Almonds, and Fig-trees; heretofore with Palmes: pleasantly rich when husbanded, and now vpbraiding the barbarous with his neglected pregnancy. [Pp. 198–9]

Cairo had appeared under the same aspect:

> Hither the sacred thirst of gaine, and feare of pouerty, allureth the aduenturous merchant from far remoued nations: by reason of the trade with *India,* and neighborhood of the Red sea. . . . Yet little is the *Turke* aduantaged thereby: slouthfull, of a grosse conceit to deuise new waies vnto profit,

and vnexpert in nauigation; which to an industrious and knowing people would affoord an vnspeakable benefit. [P. 122]

The whole region was clearly ready for new management.

Sandys's awareness of the strength and dynamism of his own culture contributes to the sense that the Holy Land has been drained of its power. At the beginning of the Third Book he calls it "A land that flowed with milk and honey: in the middest as it were of the habitable world" (p. 141). The past tense of "flowed" tells a great deal; the reservation in "as it were" is even more crucial. The notion that Jerusalem is the center of the world (a notion reflected in the medieval *mappamundi*) is held at arm's length. He has just given the latitudinal coordinates of the Holy Land; a globe cross-hatched with lines of latitude and longitude obviously cannot have a center on its surface. The cartographer and the Protestant both require that space be a neutral and universal category, with no privileged exceptions. In this context centrality can be nothing but a metaphor.

Once meaning has become metaphorical it is open to transference. The Third Book opens with a subtle decentering, the Fourth with a massive transposition, as Sandys turns his back on Acre and faces West.

Now shape we our course for England. Beloued soile: as in site

——Wholly from all the world disioyned:

Virg. Ecl. 1

so in thy felicities. The Sommer burnes thee not, nor the Winter benums thee: defended by the Sea from wastfull incursions, and by the valour of thy sonnes from hostile inuasions. All other Countries are in some things defectiue, when thou a prouident parent, doest minister vnto thine whatsoeuer is vsefull: forrein additions but onely tending to vanity, and luxury. Vertue in thee at the least is praised; and vices are branded with their names, if not pursued with punishments. That *Vlysses*

Who knew many mens manners, and saw many Cities:

Hom. Odys. 1.1

if as sound in iudgement as ripe in experience, will confesse thee to be the land that floweth with milke and honey. [P. 218]

England is the Promised Land, where a language of Edenic purity orders moral life[18]; it is Ithaca, the epic wanderer's goal; it is the *locus amoenus,* an Earthly Paradise where nature is in perfect balance; it is the pastoral haven for the dispossessed shepherds of Virgil's first Eclogue (an epic migration in lowly shepherd's weeds, which Virgil could not have foreseen); it is the unmated parent, the Mother-Father Land of its loyal sons. The insistence on England's self-sufficiency, carried to the extreme of taking up the old arguments about the evils of commerce, sounds strangely coming from a man who spent his life as a traveler, a colonial official, and a translator. Perhaps it is precisely England's increasing involvements on a global scale that inspire the attempt to create an ideal identity for her, apart from the world she was beginning to master, a nationalism which could serve as the basis for colonialism.

In any event it is a grand gesture. The Holy Land is not the center of the world but the limit of Sandys's wanderings; the invocation of England is the response to the failures of his experiences there. The juxtaposition of England with the Holy Land, as well as the reference to milk and honey, suggest a typological transference—but this transference is not enforced: it is no Puritan doctrine of a New Jerusalem, but a lighter, poetic, allusive strategy, which touches on a whole series of fundamental mythic structures, picking up power from each. They are reconciled with each other (Ulysses and the milk and honey) as they are relocated, recentered in England.

6

Italy

Book Four describes "The Remote parts of Italy, and Ilands adioyning", as the title page tells us: Cyprus, Crete, Malta, Sicily, Calabria, and only then Naples and the coast of Italy up to (but not including) Rome. About a year earlier Sandys had come over the Alps and visited the brilliant cities of northern Italy; and presumably all the heritage of humanism, spread before him at once, had dazzled him as it had so many other northerners on this secularized Italian pilgrimage. But in his book he comes from the East, and this itinerary postpones, for several reasons, the full engagement of his humanism. To begin with, the movement into the classical past (which was the normal correlative of crossing the Alps) gets lost in negotiating the military frontier. There is an evident sense of excitement and relief in seeing the barriers against the infidel—which until now Sandys has had to internalize, as intellectual and emotional resistance—take physical form again. The coast of Italy all the way to Rome was ringed with forts and scoured each night by mounted patrols. The history of Cyprus has a strong forward momentum that carries us to the climactic battle with the Turks, to climactic stories that are themselves a moral line of defense, a way of hardening the will. Their extravagant gestures and moral and emotional extremes are a way of embodying all the tension of the frontier.

> . . . the famous *Famagosta* was erected by king *Costa*, as they say, the father of Saint *Katherine*. Eternized by the vnfortunate valour of the *Venetians*, and their auxiliary forces, vnder the command of *Signior Bragadino*, who with incredible fortitude withstood the furious assaults, made by the populous army of *Selimus* the second, conducted by Mustapha: and after surrendred it vpon honourable conditions, infringed by the periured and execrable *Bassa*. Who entertaining at his tent with counterfeit kindnesse the principall of them, suddainly picking a quarell, caused them all to be murdered, the Gouernour excepted, whom he reserued for more exquisite torments. For hauing cut off his eares, and exhibited him by carrying of earth on his backe to the derision of the Infidels, he finally fleyed him aliue; and stuffing his skinne with chaffe, commanded it to be hung at the maine yard of his Galley. [P. 219]

. . . in the heart almost of the Iland, and midst of a goodly plaine, stands the late regall City of *Nicosia;* circular in forme, and fiue miles in circumference: not yeelding in beauty (before defaced by the *Turke*) vnto the principall cities of *Italy.* Taken by the foresaid *Mustapha* on the ninth of September, in the yeare 1570 with an vncredible slaughter, and death of *Dandalus* the vnwar-like Gouernour. The chiefe of the prisoners, and richest spoiles, he caused to be imbarqued in two tall ships, and a great Gallion, for a present to send vnto *Selimus:* when a noble and beautifull Lady, preferring an honourable death, before a life which would proue so repleate with slauery, and hated prostitu-tions; set fire on certaine barrels of powder, which not onely tore in peeces the vessels that carried her, but burnt the other so low, that the sea deuoured their reliques. [P. 220]

Malta is Sandys's first landing, and it is the first line of defense. Nowhere in the *Relation* is there a stronger sense of homecoming than in the satisfaction with which he surveys the island, where a militant European Christendom displays itself in its most noble and stirring shapes. The new fortified city of Valetta, the organization, pageantry, and exploits of the Knights of Malta, even the episode with the nymphs on his arrival (see Chapter 2) are all rendered with a new sharpness and energy.

Malta is almost the first place Sandys shows us that is not dominated by its ruins; history there means current geopolitics. More surprisingly, Sicily is not dominated by its ruins either, though Sandys has a rich understanding of its history. Its cities are vigorously alive in the present. There may not really be more to see here than in the Muslim world, but he is more willing to see it and be appreciative. He can talk to the natives, and so the people he meets and the stories they tell are included in his text, something that almost never happens farther east. As he is rowed from Messina to Calabria he has an uncharacteristic fit of garrulity.

Here a certaine *Calabrian* hearing that I was an *English* man, came to me and would needs perswade me that I had insight in magicke, for that Earle *Bothel* was my countryman, who liues at *Naples,* and is in those parts famous for suspected negromancie. He told me he had treasure hidden in his house: the quantitie and qualitie shewne him by a boy, vpon the coniuration of a Knight of *Malta:* and offered to share it betweene vs, if I could helpe him vnto it. But I answered, that in *England* we were at defiance with the diuell, and that he would do nothing for vs. [P. 250]

All of this distracts him from the classical past: there is much to do besides digging for ruins. Besides it is hard to find the foundations of humanism in ground that is so unstable geologically, so given to erupting and eroding. We hear about Sicily being violently disjoined from the mainland; about eruptions of Aetna, the volcanic Aeolian Islands, Vesuvius, and the New Mountain; about the hellish steaming floor of Vulcan's Court near Puteoli; about strange caves (St. German's Stove, Charon's Cave) and strange lakes (Avernus, Acheron). It is a spooky landscape, where subterranean forces burst up to the surface. They are merely geological forces to Sandys, who defies the devil, but he recounts the myths and legends—Catholic as well as pagan—which riddle the terrain with entrances to a nether world. The Court of Vulcan

is said by the Romane Catholicks to be disquieted with diuels: and that the fire vnderneath, is part of Purgatory, where departed soules haue a temporall punishment. The Friers that dwell hard by in the Monastery of Saint *Ianuarie*, report that they often do heare fearfull shreekes and gronings. They tell also a late story of a certain youth of *Apulia*, a student in *Naples;* who desperate in his fortunes, aduised with the diuell, and was perswaded by him to make him a deed of gift of himself, and to write it in his owne bloud; in doing whereof he should in short time recouer his losses. Beleeuing the Deluder, according to appointment he came vnto this place with that execrable writing: when affrighted with the multitudes of diuels that appeared vnto him, he fled to the aforesaid Monastery, and acquainted the Prior with all that had happened. He communicated it to the Bishop (now or late liuing) who informed the Pope thereof: by whose command he was cast into prison, and after condemned to the gallies. Possible it is that this may be true; but *Damianus* the reporter (though a Cardinall) might haue had the whetstone, if he had not alledged his author: who telleth of a number of hideous birds which accustomed to arise from hence on a sodaine in the euening of the Sabboth; and to be seene vntill the dawning of the next day; stalking on the tops of the hills, stretching out their wings, and pruning their feathers; neuer obserued to feed, nor to be taken by the art of the fowler: when upon the croking of a rauen that chaced them, they threw themselues into these filthy waters. Said to be damned soules, tormented all weeke long, and suffered to refresh themselues on the Sabboth, in honor of our Sauiours resurrection. This he reports from the mouth of the Archbishop *Vmbertus*. But if this be hell, what a desperate end made that vnhappy *German*, who not long since slipt into these fornaces? or what had his poore horse committed, that fell in with him, that he should be damned; at least retained in Purgatory? The matter that doth nourish these subterranean fires, is sulphure and Bitumen.
[P. 269]

It is easy enough to laugh off the modern superstitions, but the ancient beliefs are harder to dispose of. The dark myths are powerfully expressed by the poets, creating a psychological density that Sandys's disbelief and sarcasm cannot dispel. This is not the aspect of ancient culture that appeals to a Christian humanist. The Catholic devils are ridiculous; the pagan gods are a delusion; but finally a devil has to be postulated behind those delusions, even if he is a rather abstract devil with no very concrete reality. Avernus

was supposed the entrance into hell by ignorant Antiquity: where they offered infernall sacrifice to *Pluto,* and the *Manes,* here said to giue answers. For which purpose *Homer* brought hither his *Vlysses,* and *Virgil* his *Æneas:*

[here he quotes sixteen ominous lines from the *Aeneid*, Book 6, on the sacrifice to the infernal dieties]. . . . And fained they were to haue descended into hell at this place: for that here those caues were, by which the infernall spirits, by the powere of magicke euoked, were imagined to ascend. As the diuell deluded those times, so do diuers these; who affirme, that Christ from hence made his triumphant resurrection. . . . Former ages did abstaine from the vse thereof; for that defiled with humane bloud, here wickedly shed in their diuellish sacrifices: and that *Styx* was supposed to flow from thence. . . . When the woods about it were cut downe by *Agrippa*, an image was found (supposed to be the image of *Calipsus*), that swet as if endued with life. And no maruell though the diuel were troubled with the dissolution of such impious customs. [Pp. 279–81]

Whether the resonances of "deuillish" are primarily theological or moral, Sandys has to face a whole side of the spiritual life of antiquity that is entirely unacceptable to him.

An ambivalence about pagan religion and mythology runs throughout the *Relation*. At the beginning of the Fourth Book he calls Venus a "goddesse of viciousnesse" as he sails past her ancient dominion of Cyprus. On the other hand there are of course all the interpretative methods for rescuing the gods, of which Euhemerism is by far the most important in this last book. It is continuous with his search for the historical origins of civilization. The gods appear most often in the guise of culture heroes, an enlightened interpretation that makes them a progressive historical force, suppressing their immorality, and liberating them from the confines of cult worship, whether as religious powers or as Euhemeristic figures in political myths (as founders of families, cities, nations, or whatever).

The progenie of the *Painim* Gods were borne in this Iland [Crete], to whom diuine honours were ascribed: to some for their beneficiall inuentions, to others for introducing iustice amongst men, repulsing of iniuries and violence, cherishing the good, deterring the bad, suppressing by force of armes the tyrants of the earth, and releeuing the oppressed. But that they were no other than mortals, the *Cretans* themselues do testifie, who affirme that *Iupiter* was not onely borne and bred in their countrey, but buried, and did shew his Sepulcher (though reproued by *Callimachus*)

(Still lying Cretans, sacred King, dare rere
Thee a tombe; thou euer liu'st and art each where.)

on the mountaine *Lassia;* as fostred in *Æginius* by the *Curetes*, which lieth on the South of *Ida:* concealed and deliuered vnto them by his mother, to preuent his slaughter. For *Saturne* resolued to destroy his male children, either hauing so compacted with his brother *Titan,* or to preuent the prophesie, which was that his sonne should depose him. A cruelty vsuall amongst the *Grecians* it was (and therefore this not to be held for a fable) to expose the infants whom they would not foster, vnto the mercie of the Desarts. [P. 225]

Some of the difficulties of Sandys's handling of Egyptian myths are here too. When he writes "But that they were no other then mortals the *Cretans* them-selues do testifie" he is clearly falsifying the Cretans' logic: for him (and for Callimachus) there are mortal men and figures for the divine that must be immortal; he has no room for the Cretans' category of the divine-but-mortal. And in the last sentence his use of the word "fable" creates problems. The point of Euhemerism is to find an historical interpretation for fables, but here "fable" seems to stand in absolute opposition to historical truth. The splintering off at this juncture of a purely negative meaning of "fable" argues for a poor or at least unintegrated understanding of the relation of fabling to its historical con-text—even as it points to that relation. As in the opening sentence of this passage, where the progeny of the gods seem to be born into their divinity but then have divine honors ascribed to them, the relations between the original event, the feigning or ascribing by the Cretans (whether deliberate or not is unclear), and the sort of interpretation applied to the resulting story, are all very uncertain.

These problems recur in Sandys's marvelous reading of the Sirens. He is rowing towards Naples, past the famous university on the bay of Salerno, and then around the headland,

> formerly called the Promontory of *Minerua:* where also stood a renowned *Atheneum;* flourishing in the seuerall excellencies of learning and eloquence. In so much as from hence grew the fable of the *Sirens,* (fained to haue inhabited hereabout) who so inchanted with the sweetnesse of their songs, and deepnesse of their science: of both, thus boasting to *Vlysses:*
>
>> Hither thy ship (of Greekes thou glorie) stere:
>> That our songs may delight thee, anker here.
>> Neuer man yet in sable barke sail'd by,
>> That gaue not eare to our sweete melodie,
>> And parted pleasde his knowledge bettered farre.
>> We know what Greekes and Troians in Troys warre
>> Sustained by the doome of Gods: and all
>> that doth vpon the food-full Earth befall;
>>
>> Hom. Od. l.12

the same attributes being giuen vnto them which were giuen to the Muses. But after that these students had abused their gifts to the colouring of wrongs, the corruption of manners, and subuersion of good gouernment: the *Sirens* were fained to haue bene transformed into monsters, and with their melody and blandishments, to haue inticed the passenger to his ruine; such as came hither, consuming their patrimonies, and poisoning their ver-tues with riot and effeminacy. [P. 251]

The Sirens appear first as culture heroes, the human analogues of the Muses, the exponents of the arts most dear to the humanists: eloquence and history. But rhetoric is a notoriously ambivalent power, and out of that ambivalence Sandys creates a story of the degeneration of the art and of the artists. This story—whose theme is ultimately the freedom of the will to use or abuse its human powers, a choice reflected in cultural institutions and cultural history—is substituted for the Greek myth of the Sirens' hubristic competition with the Muses in a singing match. It is precisely Sandys's ability to shift the context of the myth, to fill Homer's lines with an unlooked for meaning, that makes this such a fine interpretation; but the reverse of *that* power is anachronism. We are required to believe that a university had flourished and degenerated by the time Ulysses sailed by.

There are some more effective integrations of myth into history, like the Cyclopes, who are submitted in orderly fashion to Euhemerism, archaeology, and an anthropology of primitive survivals. But in general historical understanding of the archaic, as of the foreign, is piecemeal and external; imaginative interpretation of the text is substituted for understanding of the historical context. This is roughly the same in Italy or Egypt or Crete or Phoenicia, and it is not at all surprising. It is a hermeneutical problem, a failure to isolate and define and respect the intentions and the situations of the authors. Isolating and defining and respecting the intentions and the situations of the classical authors was exactly the hermeneutical success of the humanists.[1]

What distinguishes this last book of the *Relation* from the others is that the classical authors are so often there to help, Sandys's understanding of them allowing him to use them deftly and appropriately. I will return to this point shortly; as far as mythology is concerned it might be remarked that the Neo-Latin poets he uses to populate the coast of Italy with belated nymphs are closer to the urbane and decorative mythologizing of Ovid than Ovid is to his archaic sources. Sandys's strategy is built around a continuity of artistic understanding.

In Chapter 2 Sicily and Naples were used as examples of his reliance on native poetic traditions. The opening of the description of Sicily may serve again to show how he can use his materials in a synthesis that is more artistic (an attempt to give us Sicily whole, in a graspable and appealing form) than narrowly historical—though historical resonance is certainly a crucial artistic element. He begins, as usual, with the etymology of Sicily's name, and, as usual, this becomes a demonstration of his ability to make one thing lead to another. His way with etymologies resembles his way with myths and emblems: he is more interested in collecting all the suggestive meanings that can be drawn out of the word than in settling on a single philological truth; he may, as a philologist, prefer one meaning, but he is careful not to dispense with any. So Sicily was first called Trinacria, which calls for a geographical gloss, and then

> *Sicilia*, not (saith Scaliger) of the *Ligurian Siculi*, who expulsing the *Sicani*, inhabited in their roomes, as is for the most part beleeved; but so called of

Sicilex, which signifieth cut and selected (as *Silex* signifieth a stone that is hewne, and chosen) in that violently deuided from *Italy*,

> Or seas the earth with sudden waues ore-laid
> Or cut; and new shores of the mid-land made.
> Where struggling streames still toyle with might and maine;
> Lest flood-torne mountaines should vnite againe.
>
> Lucan 1.3.

Lucan is at hand with an artistic illustration of Sicily's etymology and geography; Ovid is equally available to help with mythology.

Sacred of old vnto *Ceres*, and *Proserpina:* for that

> The gleabe with crooked plough first Ceres rent;
> First gaue to earth corne and milde norishment:
> First lawes prescribed:———
>
> Ouid M. 1.5.

who are said here first to haue inhabited, in regard of the admirable fertility of the soyle . . . [P. 235]

Sandys's description of Sicily is a commentary woven around such materials, supporting, explaining, and integrating them, and being reinforced and enlivened in turn. It is an easy transition from Ceres to Sicily's importance to Rome as its granary to its present fruitfulness: all these aspects are drawn into a rich simultaneity that is not anachronistic.[2] The Sicily Sandys visits manages to be the same one from which Ovid's Proserpina was raped: "The boughs coole shade, the moist earth yeelds rare flowers: / Here heate, nor cold, the deathlesse Spring deuoures."

These infusions of the classical tradition begin to well up everywhere when Sandys reaches Sicily, but his historical understanding is still uneven. His handling of the histories of Sicily's cities is as classical in orientation as one could wish, but in the formal political history of the island as a whole all the depth and sense of continuity exhibited above disappear. In its flat and intricate patterning this narrative resembles the other formal historical narratives of Byzantium, Egypt, the Holy Land. Sicily is "like the ball of Discord": the recurring pattern in its history is of betrayal, insolence, and vengeance—a pattern of justice, "if iustice will countenance so bloudy a designe" (p. 237), with a cautionary moral. The values of the narrative are story values. The stories are of great men, whose actions determine the subsequent history of Sicily, but the stories open out onto a timeless dimension of ethical significance, on the one hand, and a realm of pure narrative pleasure, on the other. The island fell into the hands of the Saracens because of the treason of Prince Euphemius, who had abducted a beautiful nun: there is no sense of the rise and fall of cultures and military powers behind this narrative. There is no sense of the larger shapes of history.

There is virtually nothing from the classical period in this sketch, but in the history of Syracuse there is nothing else: we move directly from its recoloniza-tion by Augustus to the present. The whole description flows from the main current of classical civilization.

> Archias not daring to returne vnto Corinth, hauing vnnaturally abused a youth of honest behauiour, imbarqued himselfe with certaine Corinthians and Dorians, and came together with Myscellus vnto Delphos to consult with the Oracle. Demanded by Apollo, whether it were riches or sanity that they affected, Myscellus said sanitie, and Archias riches: whereupon he com-manded the one to erect Crotona, and the other Syracusa. Which he did in the second yeare of the second Olympiad. Where they in short time grew so wealthy by the fertilitie of the soile, and benefit of the hauen, that it became a prouerbiall scoffe vnto the too sumptuous, that they were not worth the tithes of Syracusa. Archias slaine by Telephus, whom he had formerly defiled; the Citizens conuerted the gouernment into an Aristocracie. But the Nobles by a law that they had made, as iealous that some of them should haue affected the tyranny, exiled one another: so that the commons assumed the gouernment. After, to accord a dangerous sedition, they chose Gelon for their Tyrant . . . [P. 239]

We begin again with a myth of origins, but a myth within historical time, and clearly in a moral dimension (or several moral dimensions: of solemn choice in a religious context, of proverbial wisdom, of a pattern of retribution). The death of the founder completes the moral pattern and inaugurates a political one, as Syracuse begins to revolve through the cycle of political forms. Syracu-san history provided an archetype of ancient political theory, and so of Renais-sance political theory; the vigorous (if also violent and unhappy) political life of this city is its distinctive legacy, and governs Sandys's consideration of it. So Archimedes is introduced as the inventor of "miraculous engines" that enabled the city to hold out against the army of Marcellus for three years, though this civic role certainly does not exhaust his significance. Sandys quotes a long epigram by Claudian celebrating his invention of a "Sphere," a moving model of the heavens, which locates him in the history of the human race and its civilization:

> When Ioue within a little glasse suruaid
> The heauens, he smil'd; and to the Gods thus said:
> Can strength of mortall wit proceed thus farre?
> Lo, in a fraile orbe my works mated are.
>
> . . . .
>
> Viewing her owne world, now bold Industrie
> Triumphs, and rules with humane power the skie. [P. 240]

The dazzled sense of decisive historical progress is the sort of thing we would expect to find in a poem addressed to Newton.

Even the works of the Tyrants can reach a certain kind of sublimity, can create the feeling that the limits of human power have been attained, whether for good or ill.

> As for the Castell *Hexapyle,* it stood further off vpon the summit of a rock; which *Cicero* doth call the great and magnificent labour of Tyrants: consisting of solide stone, and raised of a wonderful height, more strong then which there could be nothing made, or almost imagined. All being defaced by *Marcellus,* and suffering a further destruction by *Pompey.* . . . [P. 241]

The works and the ruins are both exemplary, though in different senses; in fact for Sandys history might be said to be the clash of those two senses, a sublime but unromantic alternation of achievement and mortality. It is an alternation that informs the cycles of Syracusan politics, and includes both the tyrants' fort and Archimedes as the embodiment of creativity. It reaches its most concentrated expression in the famous story of Archimedes' death:

> When the Citie was taken, a souldier found him in his study, busie about certaine Geometricall proportions; who ready to strike, desired him a little to stay vntill he had perfected his demonstration: who forthwith slue him, offended with his answer; to the much grief of *Marcellus,* who not onely spared his kinsfolks for his sake, but had them in great honour. [P. 240]

This is a perfect story: it has been pared down from Plutarch's rather undirected amplitude to its most schematic form without losing any of its essential features. We have three sharply realized dramatic characters, embodying three cultural forces—Archimedes, the abstracted and completely human mathematician; the anonymous soldier, a murderous automaton; and Marcellus, who mediates between them, a noble soldier who understands the value of honor and culture, who tries to preserve the relics. It is a luminous action, that goes to the heart of the dynamic of history as Sandys understands it—a myth in the most significant sense of the word.

To write history, then, is to tell the story of civilization, from the works of the deified inventors to the founding of cities, the accomplishments of men like Archimedes, and the refinement of sensibility in the classical writers. It is also to mobilize the will and steel the nerve for the hard labor and inevitable failures civilization requires—to deliver threatening instructions. Insofar as history is concerned with the limitations as well as the possibilities of the human condition—and in large part it is, for Sandys, though finally he does not seem pessimistic—it tends, as in the story of Archimedes, to take on a timeless quality. Even the story of progress is not cast as such: the intention seems to be to commemorate the deeds of worthy men or the greatness of particular civilizations, a very different project. History is a field in which the will exercises itself, a public, exoteric, strenuous matter played out in a series of concrete situations. Any larger designs are almost entirely implicit. There is nothing like an explicit theory of historical progress.

This is virile history on a classical model. Of all the forms of historical understanding Sandys entertains it is the most resistant to any sort of occult patterning, such as the symmetries and prophecies surrounding the fall of Byzantium. The theological context of Turkish history is the most hospitable to such ideas; elsewhere it has been shown how Sandys mutes the hermetic reading of Egyptian history, and how in the Holy Land the divine operates in history almost exclusively as a negative force that is conspicuous by its withdrawal. Yet in the midst of the discussion of the secularization of the formal history of the Holy Land intruded Sandys's extraordinary quotation from the *Sibylline Oracles*. This is as occult as one could wish. Sibyls had been surfacing as early as Book 1:

> *Samos* doth also challenge one of the *Sibyls*, whose name was *Pytho*, and *Heriphyle*: and flourished in the dayes of *Numa Pompilius*; of Christ thus prophesying:
>
>> Thy God thou foolish Iuda knewst not; knowne
>> Not vnto earthly minds: but crowned hast
>> His browes with thornes, and giuen him gall to taste. [Pp. 88–89]

The Sibyls' attraction for Sandys is as great as the promise they hold out. They were everywhere, at Troy before and after the Trojan War, informing Homer's poetry[3] as well as Virgil's, both in the Aeneid and the fourth *Eclogue;* they "sung the Roman destinies," and provided Rome with an oracle; most importantly, they foretold Christ; and Sandys seems half ready to credit them with foreseeing the Turkish conquest of Rhodes in 1522:

> Vnto this lamentable subuersion (though meant perhaps by a former) may that prophesie of *Sibyls* be vnwrestedly applied:
>
>> Daughter of Phoebus, Rhodes, long shalt thou raigne:
>> Abound in wealth, and rule of seas obtaine.
>> Yet forc't by those that couet thee, at last
>> Yok't shalt thou be, rich-faire, for glory past. [Pp. 91–92]

They seem to hold a privileged point of historical vision, a sort of Merlin's glass where all times and places give onto one another. They oversee and participate in the continuity of classical civilization from pre-Homeric times to the burning of their books in Rome in the days of Theodosius the younger; and of course they establish a crucial continuity between classical civilization and the divine history of Christ. If Euhemerism is a way of giving the classical gods a legitimate and valuable role in the history of civilization, a role that is independent of sacred scripture,[4] the Sibylline prophecies allow for a greater claim for classical culture as embodying not only human values but also an independent revelation. In the Middle Ages the Sibyls were accepted as parallel to the Prophets, a parallel expressed visually in the cathedrals where they were virtually the only representatives of the classical world.[5] In his history of the Holy Land Sandys actually prefers the sibylline revelation to the Judaic one, his attraction to the recovered classical world increasing his stake in the matter. The Sibyls would introduce an order into the world's history, and one based in the classical tradition.

So when he comes to the cave of the Cumean Sibyl he gives the whole matter close and serious attention for several pages. He begins with an account of the manner of her prophesying that is both an analysis and an evocation, with abundant documentation from the Third and Sixth Books of the *Aeneid:*

> It is reported of these *Sibyls,* (for many of them there were, and that was a generall name to them all) that they vnderstood not themselues what they had said, nor remembred it: deliuering their Oracles in rude & vnpolished verse, obscurely, and perplexedly; being vttered out of a phrantick fury when possessed by the spirit. . . .
>
> > Yet brooking Phoebus ill, about slings she,
> > Distraught: her breast striues from his power to free.
> > The more her forward tongue he forces; tames
> > Her sturdy heart: and both to his will frames.
>
> Such turbulent extasies proceeded without question from a diabolical possession. But surely a peaceable, and better spirit did inspire them with those heauenly diuinations of our Sauiour . . [P. 284]

The attention to the appearance of the revelation, to its decorum, begins as a way of obtaining detailed historical knowledge, but it turns out to have spiritual implications, to reveal a spiritual incompatibility. For once Christian truth in a pagan garb is unacceptable, a breach of decorum, rather than something to be aimed at. This may be the same Sibyl that foretells Christ, but Sandys requires not only a different source of inspiration but a meekly Christian demeanor. The Sibyls did not understand their own words; if they offer a key to history, it is not in the form of a rational, transcendent *logos.* They are nearly as obscure as history itself. Usually they did not illuminate their visitors, but sent them away cursing: "To seeke in sought-for Fate / They thence depart; and Sibyls mansion hate. *AEn.* 1.3" (p. 283).

Virgil's Sibyl will not do, so Sandys turns to the text of the *Sibylline Oracles.* But as the continuity between Virgil's Sibyl and that of the *Oracles* has broken down, so the *Oracles* themselves disintegrate as he brings the techniques of textual analysis to bear on them. He never quite gives up the idea that the Sibyls prophesied Christ, but he is driven back to nothing but a rather oblique reference at the beginning of the fourth Eclogue:

> that prophesie of our Sauiour by this of *Cuma;* borrowed from her by *Virgil* (as he confesseth) though perhaps not applied by him where it was meant, but left at random to be construed by euent, and mixt with fiction. [P. 284]

What he can believe in is something behind Virgil which cannot be seen, like the *prisca theologia* thought to lurk behind Greek and Latin poetry.[6] When it is seen there are problems with decorum; when it is analyzed it falls apart. The tradition which promised to insure continuity proves to be discontinuous itself, really several traditions.

> This is she that foretold of the destruction of *Troy,* and withall of the inuentions of *Homer:* who hath inserted sundry of her verses into his poems. And said to be she that sung the *Roman* destinies. But I cannot beleeue that this was that *Sibylla* (although she be called long-liued) that brought those nine bookes to sell vnto *Tarquinius Superbus.* [P. 286]

The great promise of the Sibyls has failed, has disintegrated into bad texts and an untrustworthy tradition, scattered leaves. This is a perfect example of Frances Yates's Latin humanism getting the better of the attractions of the occult. Finally Sandys remains firmly committed to critical textual analysis, and to the differentiation of epochs that philology fosters. This committment is decisive: it finally clears the ground for a presentation of classical civilization in purely humanist terms.

The strength of this last book lies in its familiar grasp of Roman history, and in particular Roman social history at the moment when, at the height of the power of the Empire, corruption began to work on private as well as public life. It is the moment of failure, when there was most to lose, when the great moralists—Horace, Seneca, Juvenal—were there to castigate the degeneracy growing around them. The greater part of Sandys's description of the Italian mainland is taken up with the area around Puteoli, "whose ruines do yet affirme that prodigality and luxurie are no new crimes, and that we do but re-do old vices" (p. 262). This was the playground of the Empire, where its decadence and immorality and hubristic overreaching were given their fullest expression. Baiae is the epicenter of this degeneracy, "The Inne (saith *Seneca*) and receptable for vices: where luxury taketh the reignes, and is (as in a priui-ledged place) there far more licentious . . ." (p. 291), but exemplary ruins are scattered everywhere. Caligula built a bridge over the bay of Baiae, "(a prodi-gall, and not to be exemplified vanitie)"; and in the course of his triumphal opening of it, "calling many from the shore, he caused them all to be tumbled from the bridge for his cruell pastime: and those to be beate off with oares and staues, that endeuoured their owne safetie. Such were the monstrous follies,

and barbarous delights of this monster" (p. 274). Nero tried to build a canal
between Ostia and Avernus:

> *Seuerus* and *Celeris* were the ouerseers of the worke, and the contriuers; men
> of wit and impudency to attempt by Art what Nature had prohibited. They
> began to dig through the adioining mountaines, which yet retaine the im-
> pression. A lasting monument of ouerweening hopes, and franticke pro-
> digalitie. [P. 282]

Baiae offers any number of lurid stories, but Sandys's handling of it is not
easy, knee-jerk moralizing. He also sees what was magnificent about it, and its
degeneracy is something he understands intimately and historically. The hanging baths and rooftop pools have an inventor, the same Sergius Oratus who was
the first to build pits for oysters around his house. We hear a great deal about
the fashion of keeping lampreys, which is an occasion for illustrating the folly
and fatuity and conspicuous consumption of Baiae. They have uglier associations as well: the lampreys

> haue bene of diuers incredibly affected: inso much as *Crassus* bewailed the
> death of one, no lesse then the losse of a sonne; and built a sepulcher for it.
> *Caius Hirtius* who had a Mannor house also in *Baiae*, was the first that
> inuented these stues for Lampreys; who receiued for the houses which were
> about his fish-ponds, two thousand Sestertians; all which he spent in food
> for his fishes. . . . The Tyrants of those times (nor was *Augustus* free from
> that sauage pastime) tooke a delight to throw the condemned into these
> ponds, to be deuoured by them; because they would see them torne in peeces
> in an instant. [P. 293]

Sandys dwells at length on the amphitheater at Puteoli: again his horror is
informed by a detailed knowledge of the institution, whose history reflects the
progressive decay of Roman morals.

> Sword players (who were first introduced by *Iunnius Brutus* in the funerals
> of his father) first begun with staues, and then with swords, to shew their
> arts and courages. But in latter times they entred the lists naked: their skill in
> defence, not so much regarded or praised, as the vndanted giuing or receiu-
> ing of wounds; and life vnfearfully parted with. . . . *Nero*, that enemy of
> mankind, exhibited foure hundred Senators, and six hundred Knights in
> those disgracefull combatings. And *Domitian*, that other monster, produced
> women to vndergo the like in the night. . . . Histories not onely affirme that
> the Emperor *Commodus* did play the Gladiator; but his statue in this fash-
> ion, yet to be seen at *Rome*, in the Pallace of *Fernese*. [P. 270]

What appalls him most—and what bears emphasis in his evaluation of what
went wrong in Roman society—is not so much the cruelty itself as the element
of perversion. So tragedy becomes pornography when it is played by condemned men who will really die:

> But o the wicked delight of these barbarous Tyrants, worthy to suffer what they inflicted! who caused miserable wretches to make histories of fables, and put in act imaginary miseries. They most praised of the dry-eyed beholders, that exposed themselues vnto death without terror: either by taking it from the weapon of another, or by falling on their owne; as the fable required. Nor mattered it who had the part to suruive, he being but reserued for another dayes slaughter. And sometimes they erred in the story to make the catastrophe more horrid . . . [P. 271]

And so Roman valor and Stoic self-control degenerate into mere spectacle; the end of the tradition is so degraded that we can only feel relief when a "barbarian" king puts an end to it.

> *Theodoricke* King of the *Goths*, did vtterly abolish these execrable pastimes. For what could be more inhumane, then to give the condemned life, that they might take it from each other by mutuall slaughter? . . . The relicks of this is now ouergrowne with briers and thornes . . . [P. 272]

The amphitheater, the hippodrome, the theater—Puteoli has one of each, and each time Sandys seizes the opportunity to describe the whole institution, giving its history and describing other structures in Rome. These were the places where Roman society displayed itself to itself in its decadence—and in each case Nero holds the center stage, as patron of the murderous spectacles in the amphitheater, as an actor in the public theaters, as a charioteer in the hippodrome. He appears and reappears in Baiae as a guest in its pleasure palaces, as the object of a conspiracy, as the ghastly murderer of his own mother. He is the monstrous epitome of a civilization grown monstrous.

"We will not speake of the rootes of the hils here hollowed by *Lucullus;* for which called gowned *Xerxes* by *Tubero* the Stoick" (p. 300): each stone seems to have some such story attached to it. Puteoli with its *exempla* of gluttony, prodigality, hubris, greed, and cruelty is a kind of negative reflection of the Holy Land with its scenes of martyrdom. The difference—and it is a difference from the *exempla* gathered in Turkey and Egypt as well—is the willingness and ability to know the situation in depth and detail. Here the moral tales are part of social history, a wider ethical context. And, partly as a consequence, the stories have a fuller fictional form, are clothed in a richer fabric, and are all the more effective for it. Many of the examples I have quoted—Caligula's bridge, Baiae, the amphitheater, and others (even the stories from the fall of Cyprus)—show the same momentum towards realizing a moral extreme in an extreme situation, a dramatic scene, which is brought before our eyes with great force and particularity.[7]

The patience of these reconstructions is all the more extraordinary given that Sandys sees so little that pleases him, so few of the examples of the culture that initially inspired the humanists to the work of recovery on which he draws. But he looks for a *via media* between the demonic and the degenerate, and he can find it even in the vicinity of Puteoli: it takes him past Cicero's villa, and the ruins of ancient Cuma, whose Greek founders governed "their flourishing Commonwealth with the wise and honest *Pythagorean* discipline" (p. 282), and to a reposeful afternoon among the ruins of Puteoli.

Neptune was of this city the Patron: the ruines of whose Temple are yet to be seene, hard behind the Duke of *Toledos* orchard, where we refreshed our selues during the heate of the day. A place of surpassing delight: in which are many excellent statues, recouered from the decayes of antiquity; and euery where fountaines of fresh water, adorned with Nymphs and Satyres: where the artificiall rocks, shells, mosse and tophas, seeme euen to excell that which they imitate. [P. 272]

For the moment Italy is making good on all her promises to the humanist. A little later there is again an untroubled excitement at the fecundity of the soil, at the wealth of antiquities waiting just beneath the surface:

The plaine that lies betweene these hils and the Citie, is repleate with ruines: where are to be seene the foundations of Temples, Theaters, &c. vnder which, no doubt but many admirable antiquities haue their sepulture. Approved by that triall made by Alphonsus Pimentellus the Vice-roy. . . When hauing remoued but the vpper earth, it was their chance to light on an entire Temple, although crushed together: the walls and pauement of polished marble, circled with a great *Corinthian* wreath, with pillars, and Epistals of like workmanship; together with a number of defaced figures excellently wrought: the worke as well of the *Grecians* as *Latines*. There they also found the statue of *Neptune*, his beard of a blew colour: of *Saturne*, of *Priapus* (for he held in his hand the heft of a cycle:) of *Vesta* with the top of her haire wound round in a fillet . . . [P. 287]

But it is the classical writers, much more often than archaeology, that put him in touch with the civilization he is searching for. Partly this is because when faced with ruins he does not question them closely, but moves instead to establish a connection with a literary source, which provides the energy and direction of his treatment.[8] This passage is the great exception; but even here he falls back on the simplest of techniques, in the absence of a literary source, simply matching up the statues with the best known attributes of the gods, in precisely the manner of an artist's handbook.[9]

But more importantly, his preference for the writers is a result of inheriting their stance, their alienation from the course of history. Of course they can be implicated in unacceptable cultural positions, as Martial's *De Spectaculis* implicates him in the immorality of the games, and as Virgil becomes the *locus classicus* for the demonic possession of the Sibyl and the devilish infestation of Avernus. But if the vatic Virgil of the Middle Ages is discredited (there is a world of contempt in Sandys's question, "but who euer heard that *Virgil* was a

Magician?" [p. 263]), his moral authority is unimpaired. The devils that matter
are those that infest Caligula and Nero. Juvenal expresses Sandys's disapproval
of the hippodrome, and Horace and Seneca come to his aid in the little homily
on moderation in drinking that serves as an induction to the pleasure grounds
of Puteoli. They will censure Baiae as well. It is easy to come to terms with
religious differences when the cultural continuity is so strong. Sandys wants to
re-create the classical world because he understands how to live his cultural and
moral life in it; and it is a stimulus to that life, a rich source of examples, both
good and bad. Nero is the figure we see presiding over the history of southern
Italy, but the voice we hear is, appropriately, Seneca's.

Seneca turns up repeatedly in this last book of the *Relation:* first as a trage-
dian, for a reference to Crete in the *Hippolytus;* then for a scientific opinion on
the fountain of Arathuse; then for a line of poetry on the Promontory of
Minerva; as a moralist giving advice on drinking; as a traveler in the Grot of
Pausylipe; as a spectator in the amphitheater. Finally Sandys begins quoting at
length from the Epistles to Lucilius on Vatia's Villa near Baiae and on Baiae
itself. Seneca is the only prose writer he quotes directly, and it is easy to see
why he is accorded this honor. The letters Seneca wrote while wandering
around southern Italy in the last years of his life provide not only information
but a model for Sandys's practice as a traveler.

> Not far from this, the Mannor house of *Seruilius Vatia* presented our eies
> with her ruines. . . . Of which, and of him, thus *Seneca* to *Lucilius:* There-
> fore I perseuered the longer, inuited by the pleasant shore, which windeth
> about between *Cuma* and the mansion of *Seruilius Vatia:* enclosed on the one
> side with the sea, and on the other with the lake; affoording as it were a
> streight passage, being thickned with a late tempest. For that water, as thou
> knowest, so prouoked, doth often ouerflow, and vnites those sands, which a
> long calme disunites by reason of their siccitie. As my manner is, I began to
> looke about me, to see if I could find out anything that might profit; and
> bent mine eyes vpon the house, which sometimes belonged vnto *Vatia.* In
> this that rich Praetor (for nothing famous but for his retirement) grew old;
> and for that onely was accounted happie. For as often as the friendship of
> *Asinius Gallus,* or the hatred of *Seianus,* or in the end his loue, had destroyed
> any, (for to haue offended him, and to haue loued him, was equally danger-
> ous) men would say, *O Vatia, thou onely knowest how to liue!* yet knew not
> he how to liue, but how to conceale himselfe. Great is the difference be-
> tweene leading thy life vacantly, and leading it slouthfully. I neuer past by
> this house of *Vatia,* but I said, *Here Vatia lay buried.* Of the house itselfe, I
> can write nothing certainly: I onely know it by the outside, and as it ex-
> poseth it selfe to the view of the passenger. Two caues there are of excellent
> workmanship, both made by Art, and both alike spacious: the one neuer
> receiueth the Sunne, and the other retaineth it vntill Sun-set. A little brooke
> there runneth diuided by Arte through a grove of Plantines, deuoured by the
> sea and *Acherusia;* sufficient for the nourishing of fish, although daily taken.
> When the sea is composed they spare them: but take them when inraged with

stormes. The chiefest commodity of this place, is in that it hath *Baiae* beyond the walls: enioying the delights thereof, and sequestred from the incumbrances. This praise I can giue it, that it is to be dwelt in all the yeare long. For it lieth open to the West winds, and so receiueth them, that it detaineth them from *Baiae*. Not vnaduisedly therefore did *Vatia* make election of this place, where now growne old, he might bestow his idlenesse. But the place doth not greatly tend vnto tranquility: it is the mind that commendeth all things. [Pp. 288–89]

If one compensates for the style, which is more conversational than the *Relation*, it would be easy to believe this passage were Sandys's own. There is Sandys's attention to landscape, a readiness to consider problems of natural history, an urbane and judicious appreciation of the villa, as well as a pressure to extract a moral meaning—"As my manner is, I began to looke about me, to see if I could find out anything that might profit . . ." Once an object of moral contemplation has been located it is developed pointedly, with an eye for ethical context as well as ethical distinctions. There is perhaps a certain quiet pride in the sophistication and clarity with which the world is perceived; the style reveals a man who takes an interest in the world, of many developed kinds. Yet if the terms which lead to the description of the villa are not actually rejected, care is taken to transcend the object of attention, to use it finally as a steppingstone to moral abstraction and injunction: "But the place doth not greatly tend vnto tranquillity: it is the mind that commendeth all things." There is a continuous dialectic between involvement and detachment, between urbanity and a readiness to turn the world into a symbol, to take refuge in the mind. There is a double injunction, to transcend but not to retire. This of course is a form of the conflict that runs throughout the history of humanism, from Petrarch on, which everyone has noticed. The case of Seneca is especially poignant: by the time he composed Epistle 55 he was in deep trouble with Nero, and the end was foreseeable. In personal or political terms the implications are tragic.

But the political implications of Seneca's career are not the point here, or are only part of the point: what seems most significant about the quotation of the Epistle is that it reveals the model of the kind of urbane stoicism Sandys has been practicing throughout the *Relation*. Seneca's relationship with Nero was a failure, but his relationship with Sandys is a great success: the continuity and community of values that failed in Roman history are made good in literary history. The spirit of classical civilization is not going to rise up out of the ground, which is soaked with blood and infested with demons, but it is alive in Sandys and his literary masters. So the alienation of this last book is not as harsh or unhappy as the alienation of the previous book. Here the context is cultural, not religious; the losses that are inevitable in any involvement with history are generously compensated for by a successful Renaissance.

We could measure the success of the rebirth or re-creation or representation of the classical world in the *Relation* simply by the level of historical detail it involves, but the crucial element is surely the literary filiation, itself a sign of the ability to hear voices in a shared language, to take part in a hermeneutical exchange. The classical world speaks to Sandys in a way the other worlds through which he passed do not: the sacred voices of the Holy Land are strangely inhibited (the Bible is not used in the way the classical poets are, to give continuous vocal expression to a culture—it is an overwhelming presence, but it is almost never quoted directly); the Egyptians silently hold up their mysterious signs; the Turks are not partners in a dialogue but a spectacle to be seen, at their most glorious in the magnificent but eerily noiseless procession of the Sultan from his seraglio to Aya Sofia which so impressed all the Renaissance travellers to Istanbul.

Notes

Introduction

1. These facts are assembled from the painstaking biography by Richard Beale Davis, *George Sandys: Poet-Adventurer* (New York: Columbia University Press, 1955), and from the articles on George, his father, and his brother in the *Dictionary of National Biography* and the *Encyclopedia Britannica* (11th ed.). There is a bibliography by Davis and Fredson Bowers, *George Sandys: a bibliographical catalogue of printed editions in England to 1700* (New York: New York Public Library, 1950).

2. George Bruner Parks, *Richard Hakluyt and the English Voyages*, 2nd. ed. (New York: Frederick Ungar, 1961), p. 60.

3. Life at the top had its perils, even for courtiers as circumspect as the Sandys. Lawrence Stone names them among the aristocratic families ruined by the cost of attendance at court in the hope of royal favor, in *The Crisis of the Aristocracy, 1558–1641*, abridged ed. (New York: Oxford University Press, 1967), p. 87. One of the most spectacular examples of the way participation in the expansion of English power could bring financial disaster was provided by Cumberland, who claimed to have lost £100,000 on his eleven privateering voyages, which forced him to speed up the sale of his estates; he had, he said, "thrown his land into the sea." Stone, pp. 174–75.

4. See Philip J. Finkelpearl, *John Marston of the Middle Temple* (Cambridge: Harvard University Press, 1969).

5. "TO MASTER GEORGE SANDYS Treasurer for the English Colony in Virginia." Quoted in Davis, p. 118.

6. Grotius and Sarpi are among the heroes of H. R. Trevor-Roper's "The Religious Origins of the Enlightenment," in *The European Witch-Craze of the Sixteenth and Seventeenth Centuries and Other Essays* (1956; reprint ed., New York: Harper and Row, 1969), pp. 193–236. Trevor-Roper mentions Sandys as a disciple of Grotius, p. 216.

7. There were new editions of the *Relation* in 1621, 1627, 1632, 1637, 1652, 1658, 1670, and 1673. Samuel Purchas reprinted most of it in *Purchas his Pilgrimes* (1625); it was digested again in John Harris, *Navigantium atque Itinerarium Biblioteca* (1705). There were Dutch editions in 1654 and 1665, and a German one in 1669. In 1973 a facsimile of the first edition was produced by the DaCapo Press (New York and Amsterdam), as part of the English Experience Series; in the same year a French translation with notes by Oleg Volkoff of the part on Egypt was published as *Voyages en Egypt des années 1611 et 1612: George Sandys et William Lithgow* (Cairo: Institut francais d'archéologie orientale, 1973). All references will be to the first (1615) edition. For contemporary references to Sandys, see R. R. Cawley, *The Voyagers and Elizabethan Drama* (Boston: D.C. Heath, 1938) and *Unpathed Waters: Studies in the Influence of the Voyagers on Elizabethan Literature* (Princeton: Princeton University Press, 1940), *passim*, as well as his "Sir Thomas Browne and his Reading," *PMLA* 48 (1933): 340, and "Burton, Bacon and Sandys," *MLN* 56, no. 4 (1941): 271–73. Johnson's reading list is printed in Boswell's *Life* (London: Oxford University Press, 1970), p. 1306.

8. Davis, pp. 223–24.

9. See Eugenio Garin, *Italian Humanism: Philosophy and Civic Life in the Renaissance* (1947; Oxford: Basil Blackwell, 1965) and *Moyen Age et Renaissance* (1954; Paris: Gallimard, 1969); Donald R. Kelley, *Foundations of Modern Historical Scholarship* (New York: Columbia University Press, 1970), pp. 1–15; Myron Gilmore, *Humanists and Jurists* (Cambridge: Harvard University Press, 1963), Chapter 1; and Thomas M. Greene, *The Light in Troy* (New Haven: Yale University Press, 1982).

10. Stephen Greenblatt, *Renaissance Self-Fashioning* (Chicago: University of Chicago Press, 1980), Chapter 6.

11. Edward Said, *Orientalism* (New York: Pantheon, 1978).

12. Rowe, "Ethnography and Ethnology in the 16th Century," *The Kroeber Anthropological Society Papers*, no. 30 (Spring 1964): 3–4. On the assimilation of New World material in general see J. H. Elliott, *The Old World and the New 1492–1650* (Cambridge: Harvard University Press, 1970); but cf. also James A. Boon, "Jacobean ethnology: An East-West intercourse" in *Other Tribes, Other Scribes* (Cambridge: Cambridge University Press, 1982), pp. 154–77.

13. Boon, p. 52.

Chapter 1. Travel Literature in England

1. Richard Hakluyt, *The Principal Navigations, Voyages, Traffiques and Discoveries of the English Nation*, reprinted in 12 vols., (New York: Macmillan, 1903–6), Vol. 1, p. xxiv. The reprint is of the second edition (1598–1600). Margaret Hodgen has written a book on this unlovely tradition, called *Early Anthropology in the 16th and 17th Centuries* (Philadelphia: University of Pennsylvania Press, 1964).

2. See E. G. R. Taylor, *Late Tudor and Early Stuart Geography 1583–1650* (London: Methuen, 1943), p. 133.

3. And of course there was Montaigne, whose broodings on the new ethnographical information and the new ideas led him to a cultural relativism of a depth unknown in England; but his accomplishment was subversive, and lies in another line of development.

4. *Richard Hakluyt and the English Voyages*, 2nd ed. (New York: Frederick Ungar, 1961).

5. Hakluyt, 1, pp. xxiii–xxiv. Ptolemy's assertion had also been quoted by Richard Willes, the literary executor of Hakluyt's predecessor Richard Eden, in his *Travayle in the West and East Indies* (1577). See E. G. R. Taylor, *Tudor Geography 1485–1583* (London: Methuen, 1930), p. 41.

6. Ibid., 4, p. 441.

7. On the work of the Royal Society see R. W. Frantz, *The English Traveller and the Movement of Ideas 1660–1732* (1934; reprint ed., New York: Octagon, 1968).

8. If he could pay, the young man could take the moralist along as tutor: Hobbes went to the continent three times in this capacity, and Ben Jonson went with Wat Ralegh, with famous results.

9. See for instance *A Direction for Travailers*, translated from Justus Lipsius's *Epistola de Peregrinatione Italica* (1592); Sir Robert Dallington, *A Method for Travell, shewed by taking the view of France as it stood in . . . 1598* (1604); Baptist Goodall, *The Tryall of Travell, or (1) The Wonders of Travell, (2) The Worthes of Travell, (3) The Way to Travell* (in verse, 1630); James Howell, *Instructions for Forreine Travell* (1642); Thomas Neale, *A Treatise of Direction* (1643); Captain John Bulmer, *A note of such Arts and Mysteries as an English Gentleman, or Souldier and Traveller is able to perform* (1649). On this tradition of advice for travelers, see Clare Howard, *English Travellers of the Renaissance* (New York: John Lane, 1914).

10. *Rosalind:* A traveler! By my faith, you have great reason to be sad. I fear you have sold your own lands to see other men's. . . . Farewell, Monsieur Traveler. Look you lisp and wear strange suits, disable all the benefits of your own country, be out of love with your nativity, and almost

chide God for making you that countenance you are; or I will scarce think you have swam in a gundello. *As You Like It*, 4, 1, 20–22, 31–36, ed. Albert Gilman (New York: Signet, 1963).

11. See Hodgen, pp. 254–70.

12. In Hakluyt, 6, p. 93.

13. "The Urbane Traveller" is the title of Chapter 11 of E. G. R. Taylor's *Late Tudor and Early Stuart Geography;* and it provides the title for Boies Penrose's *Urbane Travellers 1591–1635* (Philadelphia: University of Pennsylvania Press, 1942). Unfortunately neither one of them does very much with the phrase. Penrose's book is composed of short biographies and extended paraphrases—often inaccurate—of books by Fynes Moryson, John Cartwright, Thomas Coryat, William Lithgow, George Sandys, Sir Thomas Herbert, and Sir Henry Blount.

14. Taylor, p. 144.

15. Although we may associate Renaissance travel literature with the voyages of discovery in the New World, Geoffroy Atkinson estimates that in his period of French travel literature (1480–1609) there were four times as many books on the Old World as on the New, a ratio that remained stable. There were twice as many books on the Turks and Turkey as on the Americas. *Les Nouveaux horizons de la Renaissance francaise* (Paris: Droz, 1935), p. 10. The ratio must be similar in England: France had been much more active (and hence interested) in the Americas in the 16th century, having planted colonies in Florida and Brazil.

16. Pliny contemplates the varieties of men—the human is a very vague concept for him, and gradually shades off into one-footed or headless creatures, and animals we can recognize as monkeys—and says, "These and similar varieties of the human race have been made by the ingenuity of Nature as toys for herself and marvels for us. And indeed who could possibly recount the various things she does every day and almost every hour?" (*Natural History*, trans. H. Rackham [Cambridge, Mass.: Loeb, 1942], 2:527.) There is a sense of undirected carelessness in Nature's toying, and an indifference close beneath the surface of man's marvelling—he will marvel without being expected to learn very much or to take it too seriously. Much of this feeling persists in the Middle Ages, though Christianity had imposed a firmer idea of the unity of mankind (all were sons of Adam) and allegories were found for the marvels.

17. Davis, pp. 44–90 *passim*, especially 85–86.

18. A model for Sandys may have been the Venetian *relazione*. A *relazione* was the report a Renaissance Italian diplomat rendered of his mission on his return; originally always an oral performance, in the course of the 15th century it became usual to write down and preserve the more distinguished examples. In Venice the form became more highly elaborated: in response to the wider interests of the merchant oligarchy, a general survey of the country visited was included, incorporating geographical, historical, cultural, and economic information. The *relazione* was always the highest—the most formal, considered, and analytic—of the forms the diplomat worked in. See Garrett Mattingly, *Renaissance Diplomacy* (New York: Houghton Mifflin, 1955), pp. 112–13. It was diplomatic service or something like it that the young man was trying to qualify himself for.

19. *Purchas His Pilgrimes* (1625; reprint ed., New York: Macmillan, 1905), 1:2.

20. Ibid., 8:87.

21. Parks, pp. 224, 228. On Purchas's critics, see Boon, pp. 155–56.

22. There are honorable exceptions to the rule, like Louis B. Wright, whose attention to the Elizabethan audience and its tastes keeps him balanced. Let me take this opportunity to insert his little encomium on Sandys: "Written with urbanity and discrimination, here was a book which could gain the respect of scholars and fascinate the crowd. Most preserved copies are well worn, as if they had seen hard usage. And even yet, the old book tempts the investigator to linger over its pages. Sandys was an author who deserves better of modern readers than he has received" (*Middle-Class Culture in Elizabethan England* [Chapel Hill: University of North Carolina Press, 1935], p. 545).

23. Taylor, *Late Tudor and Early Stuart Geography*, p. 143.

24. Frantz, p. 54.

Chapter 2. Literary Character of the *Relation*

1. *The Order of Things* (1966; Eng. trans., New York: Vintage, 1973), pp. 39–40.

2. E. S. de Beer, "George Sandys' Account of Campania", *The Library*, 4th ser. 17 (March 1937):460.

3. Such as this from Seneca: "Thinkest thou that *Cato* would euer haue dwelt at Mica, to haue numbered the by-sailing harlots, and to behold so many diuers fashioned boates, bepainted with diuersity of colours; the Lake strewed ouer with roses, and to haue heard the night-noises of singers?" (p. 291).

4. de Beer, "Account."

5. In *The Poetical Works of George Sandys,* edited with an introduction and notes by R. Hooper (London: J. R. Smith, 1872), 2:405.

6. A rare exception as he is caught in a storm on the coast of Palestine: "I then thought with application, of that description of the Poets, "The bitter storme augments . . . !" [Ovid, Met. 1.11] But the distemperature and horror is more then the danger, where mariners be English, who are the absolutest vnder heauen in their profession; and are by forreiners compared vnto fishes" (p. 207). The superiority of modern navigation was of course one of the major *topoi* of the quarrel of ancients and moderns.

7. See Edward Said's *Orientalism.* Jean Zuallart, who claims in his preface "Au lecteur" to be providing the first illustrations of Jerusalem and its environs (which Sandys lifts from him), tells us about them that he has "(durant nostre seiour en Tripoli, & la Nauigation, pour euiter oisiuité) mis aucunement en ordre les petits pourtraicts, que i'auois simplement marquez par poincts & raiettes, (car il n'est licite ny permis entre les Turcs, de faire aucuns dessaings) . . ." *Le Tres-devot Voyage de Ierusalem* . . . (1626). Sandys used the first, shorter, Italian version of this book, *Il Devotissimo Viaggio* (1587). An egregious failure to take such practical considerations into account is offered by Warner G. Rice, "Early Travellers in Greece and the Levant," *University of Michigan Essays and Studies in English and Comparative Literature* 10 (1933):205–60.

8. Compare Peter Heylyn's preface to his *Cosmographie:* "And though I cannot tell what effect the reading of this following Book may produce in others, yet I can warrantably say thus much of my self, that the observation of the fall of so many great and puissant Empires, the extirpation of so many, and renowned Families, the desolation of so many flourishing *Christian* Churches, as the composing of this Book did present me with (though formerly no strangers to me in the course of my studies) did more conduce to the full humbling of my soul under the mighty hand of God, than either the sense of my misfortune, or any other morall consideration which had come before me."

Chapter 3. Turkey

1. There are three good books on Medieval European views of Islam: Norman Daniel, *Islam and the West: The Making of an Image* (Edinburgh: Edinburgh University Press, 1960), R. W. Southern, *Western Views of Islam in the Middle Ages* (Cambridge, Mass.: Harvard University Press, 1962), and Dorthee Metlitzki, *The Matter of Araby in Medieval England* (New Haven: Yale University Press, 1977). For the Renaissance the standard work is still Samuel Chew, *The Crescent and the Rose: Islam and England During the Renaissance* (1937; reprint ed., New York: Octagon Books, 1965). A good deal of information can be gathered out of Geoffroy Atkinson, *Les nouveaux horizons de la Renaissance francaise,* and Robert Schwoebel, *The Shadow of the Crescent: The Renaissance Image of the Turk (1453–1517)* (Nieuwkoop: B. de Graaf, 1967). Albert Hourani, "Islam and the Philosophers of History," *Middle Eastern Studies* 3, no. 3 (April 1967):206–68, is a good, brief overview of the whole history of the meaning of Islam for the West. Other more or less useful studies include Montgomery Watt, "Muhammad in the Eyes of the West," *Boston University Journal* 22, no. 3 (Fall 1974):61–69; K. H. Dannenfeldt, "The Renaissance Humanists and the Knowledge of Arabic," *Studies in the Renaissance* 2 (1955):96–117; V. J.

Parry, "Renaissance Historical Literature in Relation to the Near and Middle East (with Special Reference to Paolo Giovio)," in *Historians of the Middle East,* ed. Bernard Lewis and P. M. Holt (London: Oxford University Press, 1962), pp. 277–89; and Henri Baudet, *Paradise on Earth: Some Thoughts on European Images of Non-European Man* (New Haven: Yale University Press, 1965). Edward Said's *Orientalism* was published as this chapter was being planned; it confirmed my thinking on a number of points and furthered it on a number of others. My analysis of the idea of distortion which runs through Sandys's treatment of the Turks resembles Said's, and would not have taken its present form without his work.

2. Compare William Lithgow on Muhammad's first marriage:

That vnhappy match was no sooner done but she repented it with teares: for he being subject to the falling sicknesse, would often fall flat on the ground before her, staring, gaping, and foaming at the mouth; so that his company became loathsome and detestable. The which begun contempt in his bed-fellow; being to him manifested, he strove (vnder the shadow of inuented lies) to mitigate the fury of her hatefull disdaine; faining, and attesting, that when he fell to the ground, it was the great God spoke with him . . . The old *Trot,* belieuing all these flattering speeches, was not onely appeased of her former conceit, but also louing him more then a husband, reuerenced him for a diuine Prophet; imparting the same vnto her neighbours and gossips . . . *Rare Adventures*(1632), p. 146.

3. See R. W. Southern on the work of John of Segovia and Nicholas of Cusa, pp. 86–93.

4. See Metlizki on "The Muslim Paradise as the Land of Cockayne," pp. 210–19: "To the Western public the Muslim garden of delight was the antitype par excellence of the Christian paradise," p. 218. The garden of the Assassins was another well-known Muslim pseudo-Paradise—see Metlitzki again, pp. 222–31.

5. Sandys calls "Auicen" a "Spaniard, and Prince (as some write) of *Corduba*"; Avicenna was born in Bukhara and spent his whole life in Persia and Transoxiana, but Averroës (ibn Rushd) was *qadi* (judge) of Cordoba. The "double truth" doctrine Sandys outlines below was attributed to Averroists by medieval scholastics, though modern scholarship has been unable to discover anyone who actually held this theory.

6. For examples see the section in Atkinson called "Les Vertus des Mahometans," pp. 211–17.

7. The same paradox informs the superb military discipline of Satan's fallen Angels in *Paradise Lost:* the Turkish trappings of Satan's tyranny (which is at once a parody of heaven and a foreshadowing of earthly dominion) are another example of the continuing identification of Islam with the Devil. Blount remarks on the works of charity resulting from superstitions about the afterlife: "This furnisheth all *Turky* with excellent *Hanes, Hospitals,* and *Meskeetoes;* this makes the best *bridges,* and *high wayes* that can be imagined, and stores them with *fountaines* for the reliefe of *passengers:* These faire works so caused, seemed to mee like daintie fruit growing out of a *Dunghill* . . ." (*A Voyage into the Levant,* p. 87).

8. Beginning with the fact that Christians drink on Sunday. *Mandeville's Travels,* ed. M. C. Seymour (Oxford: Oxford University Press, 1967), Chapter 16, pp. 100–1.

9. Hourani, p. 213.

10. It is easy to find a reflection of this in the fact that the respective ecclesiastical hierarchies of East and West never had anything meaningful to say to one another; but by 1610 Turkey had effectively become part of the political balance in Europe—it was no longer simply an alien power. In spite of all the rhetoric about the unity of Christendom, Christian powers made agreements with the Turks against one another; King James, in spite of his fastidiousness about receiving a Turkish ambassador, sponsored a roaring trade with the Levant.

11. Said uses the theatrical metaphor to describe European representations of the Oriental—see especially pp. 63–66; I am using it more in the literal sense. There were of course a number of Elizabethan and Jacobean plays with oriental settings.

12. Sandys sometimes tries to relate appearances to underlying values, with varying results. We may give two brief examples, both concerning architecture. There is a moment in the description of

Topkapi Serai when it turns into an emblematic House of Pride. It is "deuided from the rest of the Citie by a loftie wall, containing three miles in circuite; and comprehending goodly groues of Cypresses intermixed with plaines, delicate gardens, artificiall fountaines, all varietie of fruite-trees, and what not rare? Luxury being the steward, and the treasure vnexhaustable. The proud Pallace of the Tyrant doth open to the South, hauing a loftie gate-house without lights on the out side, and ingrauen with Arabicke characters, set forth with gold and azure all of white marble" (p. 32). This is hardly dispassionate, but it does increase the imaginative resonance of the passage, and does in fact suggest something of the purposes of the builders.

In a less successful passage Sandys uses the Horace poem about Baiae (discussed in Chapter 3) to explain the quality of Turkish domestic architecture: "The best of their priuate buildings, inferiour to the more contemptible sort of ours. For the Turkes are nothing curious of their houses, not onely for that their possessions are not hereditary; but esteeming it an egregious folly to erect such sumptuous habitations, as if here to liue for euer; forgetfull of their graues, and humane vicissitude: reproued likewise by the Poet, 'Thou marble hew'st, ere long to part with breath: / And houses rearst, vnmindfull of thy death.' " The Horace poem obscures more than it reveals about Turkish values: it is a substitute for finding out what the Turks would say. It is not even clear whether Sandys thinks the Turks are wise in the following Horace's precept.

13. On the importance of these ideas for humanism see especially Eugenio Garin, *Italian Humanism: Philosophy and Civic Life in the Renaissance* and *Moyen Age et Renaissance* and Nancy Struever, *The Language of History in the Renaissance* (Princeton: Princeton University Press, 1970). Said claims that the western institution of knowledge about the Orient which he calls "Orientalism" still understands its subjects in a manner vitiated by an incomplete recognition of these qualities in their histories.

14. Such is the explanation offered by G. W. Pigman, III for the fact that "a reader who turns from modern enthusiasm for the Renaissance discovery of the remoteness of the past to Renaissance philological studies and treatises on history will be singularly disappointed: theoretical awareness of change and of its significance for understanding past and present is very slight indeed" ("Imitation and the Renaissance sense of the Past: The Reception of Erasmus' *Ciceronianus*," *The Journal of Medieval and Renaissance Studies* 9, no. 2 [Fall 1979]: 156–57).

15. "The *Turkish* tongue is lofty in sound, but poor of it selfe in substance: for being originally the *Tartarian*, who were needy ignorant pastors, they were constrained to borrow their termes of State and office from the *Persians*, (vpon whose ruines they erected their greatnesse,) of Religion (being formerly Pagans) from the *Arabians;* as they did of maritim names (together with the skill) from the *Greekes* and *Italians*. . . . They haue Painters amongst them, exquisite in their kind, (for they are not to draw by their law, nor to haue the figure of any thing liuing) yet now many priuatly begin to infringe that precept . . ." (p. 72).

16. In Chapter 2. The use of the Horace poem, discussed above, is another example.

17. *Rare Adventures*, pp. 162–63.

18. See Jerome Turler, *The Traveiler*, Chapter 4, "Of the Properties of the foure principal Nations of Europe," pp. 39–45. Margaret T. Hodgen says these stereotypes were derived from the medieval encyclopedists and gives examples from Muenster, Agrippa, Boemus, Mercator, and Heylyn. In *Early Anthropology in the Sixteenth and Seventeenth Centuries*, pp. 178–81.

19. See Hodgen, pp. 213–15.

20. Bernard Lewis, "The State of Middle Eastern Studies," *The American Scholar* (Summer 1979): 366.

Chapter 4. Egypt

1. Book 10, 188–92: "But, though such intellectual vigour and love of truth flourish in my breast, yet there is nothing I would rather learn than the causes, concealed through such long ages, that account for the Nile, and the secret of its source. Give me an assured hope to set eyes on the

springs of the river, and I will abandon civil war" (trans. J. D. Duff [Cambridge, Mass.: Loeb, 1977]).

2. Cf. Browne, who is really trying to dissolve the problem in "Of the River Nilus," *Pseudodoxia Epidemica*, Book 6, Chapter 8. He uses Sandys extensively throughout this chapter. It is worth noting that this tradition of speculation is European, not Egyptian—Herodotus says: "About why the Niles behaves precisely as it does, I could get no information from the priests or anyone else. . . . Certain Greeks, hoping to advertise how clever they are, have tried to account for the flooding of the Nile in three different ways . . ." (trans. A. de Selincourt, rev. A. R. Burn [London: Penguin, 1972], p. 136).

3. Sandys is following Diodorus Siculus, 1, 96—he could also have found these ideas in Belon or third hand in Purchas. The idea of using Virgil is his own.

4. Preface to *The Wisdom of the Ancients*, in *Francis Bacon: A Selection of his Works*, ed. Sidney Warhaft (New York: Odyssey, 1965), p. 277.

5. These are Sandys's translations. One could also point to poems by Propertius (4.6 and 3.11) and Tibullus. On the anti-Egyptian propaganda campaign mounted by Augustus, see David Konstan, "The Politics of Tibullus 1.7", *Rivista di Studi Classici*, 26, no. 2 (May–August 1978): 173–85.

6. Sir Walter Ralegh, *The History of the World*, ed. C. A. Patrides (Philadelphia: Temple University Press, 1971), p. 152.

7. *Of the Interchangeable Course, or Variety of Things in the World*, trans. Robert Ashley (1594), pp. 36v–37r.

8. *A Voyage into the Levant* (1636), p. 51.

9. For one example among many see Dante, *Purgatorio*, 2, 46.

10. And Jean Bodin says the Egyptians are one of those people from whom "letters, useful arts, virtues, training, philosophy, religion, and lastly *humanitas* itself flowed upon the earth as from a fountain." Quoted in Karl H. Dannenfeldt, "Egypt and Egyptian Antiquities in the Renaissance," *Studies in the Renaissance* 6 (1959): 11.

11. See Eric Iversen, *The Myth of Egypt and its Hieroglyphs in European Tradition* (Copenhagen: Gec Gad, 1961), Chapter One, *passim*. Arnaldo Momigliano's *Alien Wisdom: The Limits of Hellenization* (New York: Cambridge University Press, 1975) is a fine short study of ancient thought about foreign cultures and its limits, though he has little to say about Egypt. See also F. E. Peters, *The Harvest of Hellenism: A History of The Near East from Alexander the Great to the Triumph of Christianity*, (New York: Simon and Schuster, 1971).

12. This too is an inheritance from classical historiography. See Momigliano, "The Place of Herodotus in the History of Historiography," *History* 43 (1958): 1–13.

13. *Giordano Bruno and the Hermetic Tradition* (Chicago: University of Chicago Press, 1964), pp. 160–61.

14. Yates, p. 163.

15. Sandys does not give us a bibliography on the subject, but he refers elsewhere in the *Relation* to most of the major Egyptological texts: Plutarch, Pliny, Ammianus Marcellinus, Diodorus Siculus, Josephus, Tzetzes ("Zetes", a 12th century Byzantine grammarian whose digression on hieroglyphs includes material from a now-lost treatise by the Alexandrian Chairemon), and Alciati. We can assume he knew the other mythographers. He uses at least one hieroglyph found in Horapollo.

16. Iversen, pp. 41–49.

17. *Isis and Osiris*, in *Moralia*, trans. Frank Cole Babbitt (Cambridge, Mass.: Loeb, 1936), 5, 8.

18. Quoted in E. H. Gombrich, "*Icones Symbolicae*: Philosophies of Symbolism and their Bearing on Art," *Symbolic Images: Studies in the Art of the Renaissance* (London: Phaidon, 1972), p. 158.

19. Iversen, p. 46; Gombrich, p. 149.

20. Iversen, p. 49.

21. See Rudolph Wittkower, "Hieroglyphs in the Early Renaissance", in *Developments in the Early Renaissance*, ed. Bernard S. Levy, (Albany: SUNY Press, 1972), pp. 58–97.

22. Iversen, p. 72. On the intersection of the vogue for collections of maxims and proverbs with that for emblems see Mario Praz, *Studies in Seventeenth Century Imagery*, vol. 1, (London: Warburg Institute, 1939), p. 20. And on the Renaissance hieroglyphs generally, see D. C. Allen, *Mysteriously Meant*, (Baltimore: Johns Hopkins University Press, 1970), Chapter 5.

23. Iversen, pp. 84–86.

24. Yates, p. 22.

25. See Nancy Struever, *The Language of History in the Renaissance.*

26. *Natural History* 36.19, trans. D. E. Eichholz (Cambridge, Mass.: Loeb, 1962), 10:85–88. Sandys must also have read Strabo 17. 137 and Herodotus 2. 148, who place still more emphasis on the workmanship rather than on the affective results. Herodotus says he was taken through the upper rooms, and his response is simply one of wonder—"it is hard to believe that they are the work of men."

27. *De Spectaculis*, 1. Sandys quotes this line on p. 132, and slants it in a Plinian direction as he expands it into a couplet: "Of her Pyramides let Memphis bost / No more, the barbarous wonders of vaine cost."

28. *Natural History* 36.16.75. The moderns can be ranged in these camps—Belon: "N'en desplaise aux ouurages et antiquitez Romaines, elles ne tiennent rien de la grandeur & orgueil des Pyramides." *Observations des plusiers singularitez*, 2, 113r. And Purchas: "But I would be loth to burie the Reader in these sumptuous Monuments, the witnesses of vanitie and osentation . . ." (*His Pilgrimage*, p. 467).

29. See Pliny, ed. Eichholz, 10:60n., and the article "Sphinx," *Encyclopaedia Britannica*, 15th ed.

30. And Pico: "The Sphinxes carved on the temples of the Egyptians reminded them that mystic doctrines should be kept inviolable from the common herd by means of the knots of riddles" ("Oration on the Dignity of Man," in *The Renaissance Philosophy of Man*, ed. E. Cassirer, P. O. Kristeller, and J. H. Randall, Jr. [Chicago: Chicago University Press, 1956], p. 250). See also Henry Reynolds's "Mythomystes," (1632), in *Critical Essays of the 17th Century*, ed. J. E. Spingarn, vol. 1 (Bloomington: Indiana University Press, 1957).

31. Gombrich, p. 159.

32. Bacon, p. 278. Sandys will call Bacon the "Crown" of mythographers. The attack in Henry Reynolds "Mythomystes" (p. 177) on the idea that the philosophy may have been inserted into the fables *post facto* is clearly aimed at this passage, though he does not name Bacon. Reynolds's work is an argument for the superiority of ancient poetry, and is thoroughly Piconian. His principal argument is that the ancient poets embodied (and concealed) the wisdom of the *prisca theologia.* This wisdom basically concerns nature: he specifically attacks moral interpretations. This sets him directly at odds with Sandys and the tendency he represents.

33. Often the key to the symbol depends on knowledge of an Egyptian custom or belief, and so bits of cultural history are carried along with knowledge of the symbol. The question here is whether the symbol is being used to gloss the custom or vice versa. None of the meanings of the Sphinx are rooted very deeply in Egypt—those of the Pyramids, for instance, are more so.

Chapter 5. The Holy Land

1. *A True and Strange Discourse of the Trauailes of two English Pilgrimes* (1620), p. 7.

2. *Le Tres-deuot Voyage de Ierusalem* 3:40–41. Elsewhere he gives practical reasons why the pilgrim should be careful always to stay with his group.

3. *Principal Navigations* 5:91–92.

4. See Jonathan Sumption, *Pilgrimage: An Image of Mediaeval Religion* (Totowa, N.J.: Rowman and Littlefield, 1975), pp. 89–94.

5. Timberlake, p. 11.

6. Teddy Kollek and Moshe Pearlman, *Pilgrims to the Holy Land: The Story of Pilgrimage through the Ages* (New York: Harper and Row, 1970), p. 103.

7. Timberlake, p. 13.

8. Timberlake, p. 29.

9. Cf. Thomas Fuller, *A Pisgah-sight of Palestine* (1650), p. 4; Palestine has been called by several names, including "The Holy Land, because our Saviours Passion was acted thereon. But fear makes me refrain from using this word, lest whilest I call the Land *holy*, this Age count me superstitious." Fuller's age—that of the Puritan Revolution—might be more liable to do so than Sandys's.

10. *Purchas his Pilgrimes*, 8:185.

11. Zuallart, 3:29.

12. Cf. the English Jesuit Richard Gibbons, who says we must see "the places where the thinges we meditate on were wrought, by imagining our selves to be really present at those places; which we must endeavour to represent so lively, as though we saw them indeed, with our corporall eyes; which to performe well, it will help us much to behould before-hande some Image wherein that mistery is well represented, and to have read or heard what good Authors write of those places, and to have noted well the distance from one place to another, the height of the hills, and the situation of the townes and villages. And the diligence we employ heerin is not lost; for on the well making of this *Preludium* depends both the understanding of the mystery, and attention in our medita-tion." Quoted in Louis L. Martz, *The Poetry of Meditation* (New Haven: Yale University Press, 1954), p. 27.

13. See Martz, *passim*, especially pp. 6–13.

14. Fuller, pp. 2–3.

15. Victor Turner discusses various forms of *communitas* as central features in any pilgrimage in "Pilgrimages as Social Processes," *Dramas, Fields, and Metaphors: Symbolic Action in Human Society* (Ithaca: Cornell University Press, 1974), pp. 166–230.

16. The coexistence of a classical map of Palestine with a Judeo-Christian one is nicely illustrated by two letters by Thomas Coryate in the little volume called *Thomas Coryate, Travailer for the English Wits* (1616). The letter to his learned friend "L.W." is full of classical references and classical learning, but in the letter "To his Louing Mother" his wanderings through Asia are always recounted with reference to the Bible (the exception to this rule being Tamburlaine). His trip also takes different forms depending on his audience. He tells his mother "I haue resoluted by the fauour of the supernall powers, to spend 4. entire yeares more before my returne, and so to make it a Pilgrimage of 7. yeares . . . ." (p. 51). But in the letter to Sir Edward Philips he says, "Yet such is my insatiable greedinesse of seeing strange countries: which exercise is indeede the very Queene of pleasures in the world, that I haue determined (if God shall say Amen) to spend full seauen yeares more, to the ende to make my voyage answerable for the time to the trauels of Vlysses . . ." (p. 54).

17. In *Principal Navigations* 5:229–30. Cf. also "Remembrances for a Factor," pp. 231–42. England's largest export commodity was textiles, but they were dyed abroad. The idea was to establish a dyeing industry in England, and so permit a more profitable trade in finished goods.

18. "If not pursued with punishments" is a necessary admission to the realities of James's reign. This is overtly a poet's England, the praising and blaming a poetic (Jonsonian?) function, not a legal one.

Chapter 6. Italy

1. On this point see Nancy Struever, *The Language of History in the Renaissance*, p. 74.

2. There are some anachronisms, as when he uses Epicharmus, Theocritus, Empedocles, Euc-lid, and Archimedes to illustrate the statement that "The *Sicilians* are quick-witted, and pleasant" (p. 237). The genetic connection between the pleasant moderns and the ancients must be very

slender. This sort of anachronism is common in the cosmographers, e.g. Heylyn. It might be noted that Renaissance theories of national characters were usually based not on race but on climatic and astrological influences—so it could be argued that any people that settled on Sicily would develop the Sicilian wit and pleasantness. Heylyn makes this argument in his *Cosmographie*, p. 20.

3. Sandys is ambiguous on this point: he says of the Cumean Sibyl, "This is she that foretold of the destruction of *Troy,* and withall of the inuentions of *Homer:* who hath inserted sundry of her verses into his poems" (p. 285). There is no mention of Sibyls in Homer—does the "who" refer to the sibyl?

4. See Jean Seznec, *The Survival of the Pagan Gods,* trans. Barbara F. Sessions (New York: Pantheon, 1953), p. 15.

5. See Emile Mâle, *The Gothic Image,* trans. by Dora Nussey from the 3rd French edition (New York: Harper and Row, 1958), p. 336. The parallel was also expressed ritually in the *Dies irae* of the Roman liturgy.

6. Incidentally, Virgil's credit as a prophet of Christ is destroyed—he becomes a fabling poet of the most irresponsible kind, distorting the truth of Christianity, turning prophecy into a random sign which will drift through history picking up resonance where it may.

7. Nancy Struever's discussion of the use of illustration in humanist histography is relevant here: ". . .illusionism is the source of historical and artistic efficacy and value since abstractions, *rationes,* are such that 'after they are assimilated, they neither make a man better nor more prudent in his affairs' (Salutati). . . . Verisimilitude is the route to verity. . . . The centrality of illusionism in Humanist historiography is a product of poetic consciousness of figure and rhetorical ideas of argument by *exemplum.* By means of rhetorical *enargeia* or *illustratio* the vision of man is focused on behavior" (pp. 75–76).

8. Archeology is an invention of the humanists but, as Roberto Weiss points out, there were always humanists whose sense of antiquity was based on its literature and who had very little interest in archaeology—beginning with Petrarch (and cf. Dante before him) (*The Renaissance Discovery of Classical Antiquity* [New York: Humanities Press, 1969], pp. 16–17, 30–31). We might add Erasmus to the list.

9. See Seznec, Part II, Chapter 3, "The Influence of the Manuals." Panofsky points out that the German humanists were very slow to respond to the aesthetic values of classical art. He quotes descriptions of newly-dug-up sculpture by an Italian, who describes it in aesthetic and affective terms, and by a German, who is interested only in iconographic information ("Albrecht Durer and Classical Antiquity," in *Meaning in the Visual Arts* [Garden City, N.J.: Doubleday, 1955], pp. 272–76). Sandys seems to pass from one technique to another. He is certainly not indifferent to the aesthetic values of the sculpture, but his long catalogue of iconographic attributes (of which we have quoted only the beginning) suggests that his vocabulary has run out.

Bibliography

Allen, Don Cameron. *Mysteriously Meant*. Baltimore: Johns Hopkins University Press, 1970.

Atkinson, Geoffroy. *Les Nouveaux Horizons de la Renaissance française*. Paris: Droz, 1935.

Bacon, Francis. *A Selection of his Works*. Edited by Sidney Warnhaft. New York: Odyssey, 1965.

Baudet, Henri. *Paradise on Earth: Some Thoughts on European Images of Non-European Man*. Translated by Elizabeth Wentholt. New Haven: Yale University Press, 1965.

Belon du Mans, Pierre. *Les Observations des plusieurs singularitez*. Paris, 1555.

Bliss, Philip, ed. of Anthony à Wood, *Athenae Oxonensis*. London: J. R. Rivington, 1813.

Blount, Sir Henry. *A Voyage to the Levant*. London, 1636.

Bodin, Jean. *Methodus ad Facilem Historiarum Cognitionem*. Paris, 1566.

Boon, James A. *Other Tribes, Other Scribes*. Cambridge, Cambridge University Press, 1982.

Botero, Giovanni. *Relationi universali*. Venice, 1597. Translated by Robert Johnson as *The Travellers Breviat, or an historicall description of the most famous Kingdomes. . . .* London, 1601.

Bowers, Fredson, and Davis, Richard Beale. *George Sandys: A Bibliographical Catalogue of Printed Editions in England to 1700*. New York: New York Public Library, 1950.

Browne, Sir Thomas. *Pseudodoxia Epidemica*. 2nd ed., enlarged. London, 1672.

Cawley, Robert Ralston. "Burton, Bacon, and Sandys." *Modern Language Notes* 56 (April 1941): 271–72.

———. "Sir Thomas Browne and his Reading." *PMLA* 48 (1933): 426–70.

———. *Unpathed Waters: Studies in the Influence of the Voyagers on Elizabethan Literature*. Princeton: Princeton University Press, 1940.

———. *The Voyagers and Elizabethan Drama*. Boston: D. C. Heath, 1938.

Chew, Samuel C. *The Crescent and the Rose: Islam and England During the Renaissance*. 1937. Reprint. New York: Octagon Books, 1965.

Coryat, Thomas. *Coryats Crudities, Hastily Gobled Vp in Five Moneths Travells. . . .* London, 1611.

————. *Thomas Coryate, Travailler for the English Wits and the Good of this Kingdom. . . .* London, 1616.

Daniel, Norman. *Islam and the West: The Making of an Image.* Edinburgh: University of Edinburgh Press, 1966.

Dannenfeldt, Karl H. "Egypt and Egyptian Antiquities in the Renaisance." *Studies in the Renaissance* 6 (1959): 7–27.

————. "The Renaissance Humanists and the Knowledge of Arabic." *Studies in the Renaissance* 2 (1955): 96–117.

Davis, Richard Beale. *George Sandys: Poet-adventurer.* New York: Columbia University Press, 1955.

de Beer, Esmond S. "George Sandys's Account of Campania." *The Library,* 4th series, 17 (March 1937): 458–65.

Devereux, Robert, Earl of Essex; Sidney, Sir Philip; and Secretary Davidson. *Profitable Instructions: describing what special observations are to be taken by Travellers in all Nations, States, and Countries.* London, 1633.

Elliott, J. H. *The Old World and the New 1492–1650.* Cambridge: Harvard University Press, 1970.

Finkelpearl, Philip J. *John Marston of the Middle Temple.* Cambridge: Harvard University Press, 1969.

Foucault, Michel. *The Order of Things.* 1966. Trans. New York: Vintage, 1966.

Frantz, Ray William. *The English Traveller and the Movement of Ideas, 1660–1732.* 1934. Reprint. New York: Octagon, 1968.

Fuller, Thomas. *A Pisgah-sight of Palestine and The Confines thereof, with the history of the Old and New Testament acted thereon.* London, 1650.

Garin, Eugenio. *Italian Humanism: Philosophy and Civic Life in the Renaissance.* 1947. Translated by Peter Munz. Oxford: Basil Blackwell, 1965.

————. *Moyen Age et Renaissance.* 1954. Translated by Claude Carme. Paris: Gallimard, 1969.

Gilmore, Myron. *Humanists and Jurists.* Cambridge: Harvard University Press, 1963.

Gombrich, E. H. "Icones Symbolicae." In *Symbolic Images: Studies in the Art of The Renaissance,* pp. 123–91. London: Phaidon, 1972.

Greene, Thomas M. *The Light in Troy.* New Haven: Yale University Press, 1982.

Greenblatt, Stephen. *Renaissance Self-Fashioning.* Chicago: University of Chicago Press, 1980.

Hakluyt, Richard. *The Principal Navigations, Voyages, Traffiques and Discoveries of the English Nation.* London, 1589. 2nd ed. in 3 vols. London, 1598–1600. Reprint (12 vols). New York: Macmillan, 1903–6.

Herodotus. *The Histories.* Translated by A. de Selincourt, and revised A. R. Burn. London: Penguin, 1972.

Heylyn, Peter. *Cosmographie. In Foure Bookes.* Oxford, 1652.

Hodgen, Margaret. *Early Anthropology in the 16th and 17th Centuries.* Philadelphia: University of Pennsylvania Press, 1964.

Hourani, Albert. "Islam and the Philosophers of History." *Middle Eastern Studies* 3, no. 3 (April 1967): 206–68.

Howard, Clare. *English Travellers of the Renaissance.* New York: John Lane, 1914.

Iversen, Eric. *The Myth of Egypt and its Hieroglyphs in European Tradition.* Copenhagen: Gec Gad, 1961.

Kelley, Donald R. *Foundations of Modern Historical Scholarship.* New York: Columbia University Press, 1970.

Kollek, Teddy, and Pearlman, Moshe. *Pilgrims to the Holy Land: The Story of Pilgrimage through the Ages.* New York: Harper and Row, 1970.

Konstan, David. "The Politics of Tibullus 1.7." *Rivista di Studi Classici* 26, no. 2 (May–August 1978): 173–185.

Le Roy, Louis (Regius). *De la Vicissitude ou variété des choses en l'univers.* Paris, 1575. Translated by Robert Ashley. *Of the Interchangeable Course, Or Variety of Things in the Whole World.* London, 1594.

Lewis, Bernard. "The State of Middle Eastern Studies." *The American Scholar* (Summer 1979): 365–81.

Lithgow, William. *A Most Delectable, and Trve Discourse, of an admired and painefull peregrination. . . .* London, 1614.

———. *The Total Discourse of the Rare Adventures and painefull Peregrinations of long nineteen Yeares Travayles.* London, 1632.

Lucan. *Pharsalia.* Edited and translated by J. D. Duff. Cambridge, Mass.: Loeb, 1977.

Mâle, Emile. *The Gothic Image.* 1913. Translated by Doris Nussey from the 3rd French edition. New York: Harper and Row, 1958.

Mandeville, Sir John. *Mandeville's Travels.* Edited by M. C. Seymour. Oxford: Oxford University Press, 1967.

Mattingly, Garrett. *Renaissance Diplomacy.* New York: Houghton Mifflin, 1955.

Metlitzki, Dorothee. *The Matter of Araby in Medieval England.* New Haven: Yale University Press, 1977.

Momigliano, Arnaldo. *Alien Wisdom: The Limits of Hellenization.* New York: Cambridge University Press, 1975.

———. "The Place of Herodotus in the History of Historiography." *History* 43 (1958): 1–13. Reprinted in *Studies in Historiography,* pp. 127–42. London: Weidenfeld & Nicolson, 1966.

Parks, George Bruner. *Richard Hakluyt and the English Voyages.* 1928. Reprint. 2nd ed. with introduction by James A. Williamson. New York: Frederick Ungar, 1961.

Parry, V. J. "Renaissance Historical Literature in Relation to the Near and Middle East (with Special Reference to Paolo Giovio)." In *Historians of the Middle East,* edited by Bernard Lewis and P. M. Holt, pp. 277–89. London: Oxford University Press, 1962.

Penrose, Boies. *Urbane Travelers, 1591–1635.* Philadelphia: University of Pennsylvania Press, 1942.

Peters, Francis Edwards. *The Harvest of Hellenism: A History of the Near East from Alexander the Great to the Triumph of Christianity.* New York: Simon & Schuster, 1971.

Pigman, G. W. "Imitation and the Renaissance Sense of the Past: The Reception of Erasmus' *Ciceronianus.*" *The Journal of Medieval and Renaissance Studies* 9, no. 2 (Fall 1979): 155–78.

Pliny. *Natural History.* Edited and translated D. E. Eichholz and H. Rackham. Cambridge, Mass.: Loeb, 1962–69.

Plutarch. *Isis and Osiris*. In *Moralia,* edited and translated by Frank Cole Babitt. Cambridge, Mass.: Loeb, 1936.

Praz, Mario. *Studies in Seventeenth Century Imagery.* London: Warburg Institute, 1939.

Purchas, Samuel. *Purchas his Pilgrimage.* London, 1613.

———. *Purchas his Pilgrimes.* London, 1625. Reprint (20 vols). New York: Macmillan, 1905.

Ralegh, Sir Walter. *The History of the World.* London, 1614. Reprint, edited by C. A. Patrides. Philadelphia: Temple University Press, 1971.

Reynolds, Henry. *Mythomystes.* London, 1632. In *Critical Essays of the 17th Century,* edited by J. E. Spingarn, vol. 1, pp. 141–79. Bloomington: Indiana University Press, 1957.

Rice, Warner G. "English Travelers in Greece and the Levant." *University of Michigan Essays and Studies in English and Comparative Literature* 10 (1933): 205–60.

Rowe, John H. "Ethnography and Ethnology in the Sixteenth Century." *The Kroeber Anthropological Society Papers,* no. 30 (1969): 1–19.

Said, Edward. *Orientalism.* New York: Pantheon, 1978.

Sandys, George. *Ovid's Metamorphosis Englished, Mythologiz'd and Represented in Figures.* London, 1632. Reprint, edited by Karl K. Hulley and Stanley T. Vandersall, with foreword by Douglas Bush. Lincoln: University of Nebraska Press, 1970.

———. *Poetical Works.* Edited by R. Hooper. 2 vols. London: J. R. Smith, 1872.

———. *A Relation of a Iourney begun An: Dom: 1610. Foure Bookes. Containing a description of the Turkish Empire, of Ægypt, of the Holy Land, of the remote parts of Italy, and Ilands adioyning.* London, 1615. Reprint. New York: Da Capo Press, 1973. Book 3, edited and translated by Oleg Volkoff in *Voyages en Egypt des années 1611 et 1612: George Sandys et William Lithgow.* Cairo: Institut français d'archeologie orientale, 1973.

Schwoebel, Robert. *The Shadow of the Crescent: The Renaissance Image of the Turk (1453–1517).* Nieuwkoop: B. de Graaf, 1967.

Seznec, Jean. *The Survival of the Pagan Gods: The Mythological Tradition and its Place in Renaissance Humanism and Art.* 1940. Translated by Barbara F. Sessions. New York: Pantheon, 1953.

Shakespeare, William. *As You Like It.* Edited by Albert Gilman. New York: Signet, 1963.

Southern, R. W. *Western Views of Islam in the Middle Ages.* Cambridge, Mass.: Harvard University Press, 1962.

Stone, Lawrence, *The Crisis of the Aristocracy, 1558–1641.* Abridged edition. New York: Oxford University Press, 1967.

Struever, Nancy S. *The Language of History in the Renaissance: Rhetoric and Historical Consciousness in Florentine Humanism.* Princeton: Princeton University Press, 1970.

Sumption, Jonathan. *Pilgrimage: An Image of Mediaeval Religion.* Totowa, N.J.: Rowman & Littlefield, 1975.

Taylor, Eva Germaine Rimington. *Tudor Geography, 1485–1583.* London: Methuen, 1930.

———. *Late Tudor and Early Stuart Geography 1583–1650.* London: Methuen, 1943.

Timberlake, Henry. *A true and strange discourse of the travailes of two English pilgrims.* London, 1620.

Trevor-Roper, H. R. "The Religious Origins of the Enlightenment." In *The European Witch-Craze of the Sixteenth and Seventeenth Centuries and Other Essays,* pp. 193–236. New York: Harper and Row, 1956.

Turler, Jerome. *De Peregrinatione, et Agro Neapolitano Libri II.* Cologne, 1574. Translated as *The Traveiler.* London, 1575. Reprint with introduction by Denver Ewing Baugham. Gainesville, Florida: Scholar's Facsimiles and Reprints, 1951.

Turner, Victor. *Dramas, Fields, and Metaphors: Symbolic Action in Human Society.* Ithaca: Cornell University Press, 1974.

Watt, Montgomery. "Muhammad in the Eyes of the West." *Boston University Journal* 22, no. 3 (Fall 1974): 61–69.

Wittkower, Rudolf. "Hieroglyphs in the Early Renaissance." In *Developments in the Early Renaissance,* edited by Bernard S. Levy, pp. 58–97. Albany: State University of New York Press, 1972.

Wright, Louis B. *Middle Class Culture In Elizabethan England.* Chapel Hill: University of North Carolina Press, 1935.

Yates, Frances. *Giordano Bruno and the Hermetic Tradition.* Chicago: University of Chicago Press, 1964.

Zuallart, Jean (Zuallardo). *Il Devotissimo Viaggio.* Venice, 1587. Translated and expanded as *Le Tres-devot Voyage de Ierusalem. . . .* Anvers, 1626.

Index